THE WAY
OF
THE MYSTIC

Insights on Devotion and Liberation

CHAD MILLEMON

Published by
Mystic Way Publishing

Mystic Way

www.mysticwaypub.com

ISBN-13: **978-0988869318**
ISBN-10: **0988869314**
Library of Congress Number: *pending*

Dedicated To the Fulfillment of our Divine Potential

'The Will of God has nothing but sweetness, grace and treasures for the surrendered soul. It is impossible to place too much confidence in it, or to surrender oneself to it too utterly. It always acts for and desires that which contributes most to our perfection, provided we allow it to act.'

Jean-Pierre de Caussade[1]

[1] From the book *The Joy of Full Surrender* by Jean-Pierre de Caussade

ACKNOWLEGEMENT

I must express eternal gratitude to everyone who
offered to help with clear feedback, creative insights
and editing suggestions.

Very special thanks to:
Kim and James Chavez, Orion Abrams, Fred Striley,
Beth Drewett, Gary Boldra, and my lovely wife
Carolyn

The following pages would not be the same without
your support!

CONTENTS

FORWARD

Years of personal practice and teaching around the world led to the writing of this book. This is an experiential manual in that it not only explains the nature of mystical experience, but also offers a means for anyone to access it. This is an outline of what can be discovered within us all.

I have no doubt that some of this material could be shared in many different ways. It is difficult, if not impossible to convey everything in a satisfactory way using words. I am under no illusion that this way is the best way for all. The best advice is to take these words as a sign pointing in a particular direction.

To argue theory is to miss the whole point. This keeps you one step removed from tasting the essence of this practice for yourself. But to a degree everyone's intellect must be satisfied and everyone's heart inspired. The point is to eventually set aside theory and instead strive toward experience - to make the transition from the restrictions of rote metallization and into the fathomlessness of the silence beyond it.

Some explanations of experiences may sound abstract. They can really only be understood for those who experience these things. Don't be quick to assume that such experiences are far from you! They are closer than you can imagine. There is nothing easier or simpler than *silence*.

Many different words here are used to describe our Divine Essence – Divinity, Self, Internal Silence, Stillness, Peace, God, etc. These are all used interchangeably. The word 'God' is avoided in some cases due to the preconceived notions many have wrapped around it. Such notions often limit one's understanding or, rather, one's *awareness* of Divinity. Many would readily agree that God is omnipotent, omnipresent and omniscient and that Divine essence is unconditional love. And yet, the strange paradox is that those same people who believe this still feel distant and separate from it - that God is somewhere out there in a vague location up in the sky and we are down here on earth. Either God is *omnipresent* or not. It cannot be both. If God is unconditional love, that is *love without conditions,* then it is we alone who put conditions in place.

You will notice that some topics and information are repeated multiple times throughout this book. Try as

I might, this couldn't be avoided. This is also the case in live teaching where key points need to be explained again and again so that they are driven home. I know as a beginning student I needed that!

Finally, many ask where the particular practice in this book comes from. The practice itself was inspired by the mechanics of a meditation practice known as 'The Ishayas' Ascension' combined with a very well known phrase borrowed from the New Testament that symbolizes the very essence of devotion to Divinity. I have offered a shorthand way of applying the practice that I have found to be powerfully effective.

At the end of the day it is one's devotion that sanctifies the action – whether that be with this particular practice or with another. One can go from one spiritual practice to another, to another and to yet another… all the while the experience of our True Essence remains the same regardless of what method is undertaken.

It is in the name of this profound indescribable Presence that I dedicate the following pages.

Chad J. Millemon
December 23, 2013

PROLOGUE

My life was once dominated by internal conflict to the degree that I couldn't imagine what it would be like to experience a single minute of peace. Deep down there was a feeling that something was missing, but I wasn't sure what that 'something' was. Since then, incredible changes have occurred in the way I perceive myself and the circumstances of my life. Previously, I couldn't imagine life *without* constant internal conflict and now I couldn't imagine life *with* it. Absorption in thought streams once obstructed peace for all but the rarest moments, now the opposite is the experience. A steady and profound silence has replaced the once dominant undercurrent of anxiety.

There wasn't an instantaneous awakening that occurred in one epic moment, where the lights all suddenly came on. My path has involved a dedicated and continuous letting go of the mind's programming. It has become clear that it is only the mind's programming that blocks the experience of peace. The letting go of all obstructions to peace has been made possible with the aid of effective techniques and guidance.

This process has been marked by a whole host of 'Aha!' moments - times in my life where I suddenly came to see things from a more expanded perspective. It was as if I was stuck in a dark box and each of these moments was like holes being punched in the sides, allowing the light to shine in.

Subtle shifts in perspective resulted from old, unrewarding thought patterns falling away. Sublime states of contentment and peace revealed themselves quite automatically, as if in proportion to the gradual decline of those patterns. There is an analogy in some Eastern teachings that mentions mistaking a rope for a snake. When the snake is perceived instead of the rope, there may be great anxiety, especially if we come close to stepping on it! But this anxiety only arises by not seeing the rope as a rope. This is a result of mistaken perception warping our view of reality - where *the world as it is* becomes clouded by *the world as I see it*. The instant the rope is seen as a rope, anxiety begins to dissolve. The physical circumstances of that moment didn't change, the consciousness of the observer did. Similarly, the real 'I' or *me* is typically not seen as it really is, but remains clouded beneath appearances that are believed to represent reality.

The true Self is known through experience as *silence*. The deeper the experience of the silence, the more the identification with what we may call 'ego-self' melts away like a grain of salt in a glass of warm water. We may define ego-self as the deep identification with the mind, body and personality. Within the purest experience of internal silence, there is no conflict to be found. Gone is the gaping hole in our hearts that tells us something is wrong, out of place or lacking in our lives. Gone is the feeling that Divinity is distant from us. Even in the very midst of noise and activity, the silence is totally undisturbed.

Doubts, limiting beliefs, and mistaken identities are all major obstacles to the direct discovery of Divine Presence in our lives. The information in this text is presented in order to help illuminate the way to peace. This book outlines a means to help us shift our attention from absorption in the field of thought and direct it toward absorption in the field of silence. Silence is not a 'thing' that is obtained or added *to* the ego-self, but rather a presence that becomes apparent with the dissolution *of* ego-self. We do not cause silence to appear with spiritual endeavor any more than the absence of fireworks causes the silence of the sky. We simply let go of whatever is blocking our awareness of it.

Contemplation, meditation or prayer may serve well to assist us in this endeavor. But only as long as we are clear and confident in our practice! To this end a powerful technique will be presented in generous detail in this text. When silence becomes apparent via direct experience, it then becomes the meditation and the prayer. The purest form of contemplation is the acknowledgment of Divine Presence in each moment.

The way to the discovery of Divine Presence is simple and direct. Any idea that it is complicated is often due to doubt, resistance or misunderstanding. All obstructions to our innate Grace can be overcome with proper tools, clear instruction and by applying these with devotion. Clear instruction helps usher in a practice that can be applied with *confidence*. This is of immense importance. If we practice any sort of meditation, contemplation or prayer while simultaneously plagued with a lingering sense of doubt or uncertainty regarding whether or not we are doing it correctly, then there will be little or no progress – like a mirage on the horizon, the goal will forever appear beyond our reach. Therefore, in terms of a valid practice, nothing short of *certainty* will do for significant progress to occur.

The way to the discovery of Divine Presence is not an intentionally held secret or mystery. Both the way and the means reveal themselves to all who sincerely seek this. The instruction presented in this book is nothing new. Like a seed that needs the appropriate conditions to sprout, the information may simply need to be placed in the proper context for it to take root and flourish in your life. Surrender of personal will to Divine Will in each moment, and at ever-deeper levels, is the purest of all paths. The human experience seems to be a constant battle of *my will be done* vs. *Thy Will be done,* with the former being more adhered to than the latter.

What are you looking for in a spiritual practice? Elaborate otherworldly visions? The secret to manifesting all your desires? Paranormal experiences? Recognition for having a special supernatural ability? Is the miraculous something *other* than what we are faced with in each moment of our lives? Is there a belief that we aren't good enough as we are, that we need to become something different to be worthy of God? Could it be that, in spite of hearing that nothing is more near to us than God, the *opposite* seems to be your experience?

If the peace of God is what you are looking for, the essentials must be extracted from the non-essentials. If we clutter our practice with false beliefs and unrealistic expectations, we waste time and energy. Many spend their whole lives dabbling in supposed 'spiritual' practices that have nothing whatsoever to do with merging personal will with Divine Will.

A glance in the 'spiritual/new age' section at a bookstore or a casual search on the Internet will yield a veritable ocean of information. For the beginning spiritual student this can lead to a bit of confusion. Where does one even begin? The purest teaching is not at all complicated, but is in fact supremely simple. Spiritual advancement and the aligning of personal will with Divine Will is by no means a new or original concept. It is the tried and true method for those rare souls who have been irresistibly pulled by grace to awaken to Reality. The pure spiritual pathway is not characterized by progression into greater complexity. On the contrary, while we may very well begin in a state of complexity, we grow into simplicity. With this particular pathway, there are not a multitude of things one needs to know or do. In fact, there is nothing easier than the Way of the Mystic.

If we aren't aligning with Divine Will then we are resisting it. Among the numerous telltale signs of resistance are anxiety, conflict, confusion, perpetual sadness, lack, emotional pain, anger, jealousy, fear, envy, greed, violence toward self and others, low self-esteem, bitterness. *Suffering in any form is a signal that personal will has taken the place of Divine Will. By contrast, uncaused joy and perpetual peace are signs of surrender to*

Divinity.

Surrender to God is at times misunderstood as an exercise in suffering. While suffering is often a great motivator for positive change, *intentional* suffering along any given spiritual pathway serves the ego rather than God. We don't need to whip ourselves to be worthy of Divinity, we only need to surrender the program that states, 'I am not worthy'. All are worthy no matter what the past has been. Our path begins anew in this very moment, which is the only moment any of us ever have.

One summer day I was invited over to a new friend's house for lunch. I was happy to see that his grandmother had a beautiful pet parrot sitting in the kitchen near the window. At fifteen years the parrot was more than twice my age. I have always had a fondness for pets and felt bad that it had to spend its life in such a tiny cage. So, I asked my friend if he ever let it out. Without hesitation he walked over, opened the cage and then came back and sat at the table to finish his sandwich. The whole time we sat having lunch the door was wide open but the parrot would not leave. It would poke its head out of the door and look around, occasionally sticking its foot out and, to my surprise, it stayed put. After about an hour my friend closed the door.

Many of us are just like that parrot. We may grow tired of the unrewarding confines of our current experience of life and desire something greater, but are we willing to let go of what is comfortable and familiar if the opportunity presents itself? We may aspire after greatness, but when the Universe reveals the means, it is up to us to choose.

INTRODUCTION

The sheer volume of religious, spiritual and new age material available these days can be confusing and even somewhat daunting for today's spiritual aspirant. It is helpful to know that the ultimate Truth has been the same throughout all of time. In spite of living in different time periods, places and within a variety of cultural and religious structures, history's great saints, sages and mystics all experienced the exact same Reality. That same Reality is just as present and equally available to all now as it has ever been.

While there is a vast amount of spiritual information available, very little of it is actually worthy of the label 'spiritual'. Pure spirituality culminates in the realization of the Presence of God within. Not only is the Kingdom of Heaven within, it is also at hand: available here and now. Few experience anything even closely resembling Heaven within. For the vast majority, inner awareness is filled with chaotic and often negative thought streams racing through the mind, dominating inner awareness. More often than not, focus is consistently projected into the past or future, leaving little awareness in the present moment. But the here and now is the only moment that anyone really has. This is the only moment that the Silence of Divine Presence can be experienced directly.

The addiction to the mind is likely the single greatest source of suffering on the planet. The potential to experience Heaven is quite literally at hand, but it seems that everyone is too busy thinking about other things to recognize it. The addiction to thinking is reinforced by repeated action and by the seeming lack of viable information regarding our True Nature. Many simply aren't aware that it is even possible to be able to experience the peace of Divinity. Some might consider such a notion absurd or even blasphemous. Some might see this as just another spiritual fad. Just as the sun is forever unaffected by clouds, Reality is immune to all mankind's mistaken perceptions, beliefs and assumptions. To deny the presence of Divinity, either consciously or unconsciously, is to live a life that is subject to suffering. *The belief that one is separate from God is the root of all human conflict.*

Very few in mankind's history have transcended separation and suffering. Those few walked a narrow path, which involves total surrender to God. All described the intense devotion that is necessary for true purification. But what does this really mean? Is this difficult or complicated? Is it beyond our reach? It would only appear as such because of misunderstanding or doubt. When the desire for Divinity is strong, all of creation, both seen and unseen, responds with absolute and unconditional support.

The terms *Divinity*, *Stillness*, *The Presence*, *Consciousness*, *Silence*, *Self* and *God* are all synonymous and refer to the exact same experience – That which has no form, no boundaries, no beginning or end. Though formless, the Presence of God is not separate from any part of the physical world of form any more than the water of the pond is separate from the reflected images on it's surface. It is the essential Reality of all that is. *The presence of Divinity cannot be fully realized, grasped, comprehended or discovered via conceptual thinking.* The mind is simply the wrong tool for the job. It is only by relinquishing attachment to the habit of conceptual thinking that God is experienced as uncaused silence, joy and love.

The feeling or belief that God is absent or distant from life is the way the world is seen from the perspective of the ego-self. It is only a false belief that views God as separate and distant, looking down upon creation from afar. Life does not need to be painstaking struggle. Only our thought processes make it so. Such mistaken notions don't create our world; they merely warp our perception of it. Most people search for God, truth, love, and fulfilment externally within the world of form. In order to know the presence of Divinity directly, it is imperative to begin to effectively direct attention *inward* on a consistent basis. All external seeking is in vain.

The habit of falling prey to the morass of internal programming over and over again is mostly innocent and unconscious. Significant spiritual work involves undoing the complex web of thought processes with which we have become heavily identified. We may refer to this web as *programming*. Our programming was set in motion by past experience and the conditioning of society. Even programs that seem insurmountable can crumble effortlessly and unravel rapidly based on the simplest of spiritual understandings.

The discovery of Divine Silence has been referred to by numerous spiritual and religious traditions as *Self-Realization, Enlightenment, Mystical Union, Awakening, Samadhi,* and *Nirvana,* to name a few. While there are many names, the experience is the same. Oftentimes, it is referred to simply as the Self. This is because mystical union with God is 100% *subjective.* It is utterly complete in its fullness and leaves one feeling entirely whole - lacking nothing. By contrast, the ego-self always perceives lack and incompletion.

Without any spiritual endeavour, consciousness typically evolves at a snails pace over very long periods of time. Some live their whole lives with little or no progression at all. Some may even regress! The world-view that is held in place at age 20 remains virtually the same at age 80. It is rare that one would even desire to question their dearly held beliefs and concepts about anything, let alone concepts regarding God. But any belief system *about* Divinity is not the same thing as the *experience* of Divinity.

PART I

THE MYSTIC

Insights on Liberation

None of the references to mystical experience in this book allude to the supernatural, astral or paranormal. This is not in denial of the existence of these realms, but they are of a different path. If given undue attention, they can serve as a serious distraction to the discovery of the presence of God. The pathway of the Mystic is defined by continuous surrendering of personal will to Divine Will. This process involves relinquishing control. We begin by looking within ourselves with a willingness to examine all our dearly held beliefs of who we think we are, what we think we know about the world and what we think God is. By being open to looking at things differently, we can begin to grow beyond whatever state we may find ourselves in. There is nothing quite so liberating as to wake up from a disturbing dream that we believed was real.

The attitude of *my will be done* will always ultimately manifest limitation and conflict in our lives. This is where personal willpower is used to get, acquire, achieve and progress, in an attempt to gain what is felt to be lacking. This is the ego-dominated worldview. It is from the perspective of the ego that external conditions appear as the *cause*, which affects our internal states of being either positively or negatively. As long as we presume that our happiness is dependent on external situations, which are subject to change, then any semblance of happiness will fluctuate right along with whatever situations that we find ourselves in. There was a particular woman who was a regular attendee at weekly meditation meetings years ago who made her living in the stock market. I never needed to check the newspaper or Internet to see how the stocks were doing when she was around. If she was happy and optimistic, her stocks were strong. And if they dropped in value, she would be angry and irritable. All too often, happiness is based on the ego's terms – 'I will be happy only if such and such happens'. This perspective is not a useful formula for finding contentment. Victim mentality allows external conditions to determine our internal degree of wellbeing.

All efforts of *my will,* no matter how noble, will forever keep one just outside the gates of Heavenly experience. God will feel distant to those who adhere to personal willpower in spiritual endeavor. It is not possible to be in control and be truly liberated at the same time. The inherent limitation of personal control is standing in our way. The feeling that something is missing in our lives follows *my will* as surely as smoke follows fire. This doesn't mean that one cannot be happy at all; it only means that we won't be permanently in a state of contentment. Anxiety is one clear indication that the agenda of *my will be done* is blocking the peace of Divinity.

Anytime we cling to concepts of God, we separate ourselves from the *Reality* of God. The notion that God is a separate entity is based in fantasy, not reality. This can be remedied by recognizing that the limited mind cannot grasp that which is infinite and eternal. This is like trying to contain the ocean in a coffee mug. To conceptualize *about* the nature of Divinity rather than acknowledging its direct presence in our lives is to indulge in mental idolatry where we mistake the thought-image for the actual thing. The more we approach God *as it is*, the less we will think *about* God conceptually.[2]

Consistently allowing *Thy Will* to be done leads to indescribable states of peace and joy. Yet, this doesn't mean that we may not experience the resistances of surrendering personal will power along the way, which may be uncomfortable. The ego's will does not

---

[2] *"…when I think on God's Kingdom, I am compelled to be silent because of its immensity…"* Meister Eckhart

always relinquish sovereignty so willingly. Old habits often fall away reluctantly, even if they are unrewarding.

This powerful teaching is simple, direct and can be applied in any moment. We must take care not to separate spiritual practice from our 'ordinary' day-to-day lives. To do so would be to miss the point entirely. The tendency to secularize our practice only perpetuates the appearance of separation. No such distinction exists in reality. Family, taxes, debts, relationships, household chores and workplace obligations should not be viewed as separate from devotional endeavor. The application of the great teachings involves a shift in perspective regarding how we relate to the circumstances in each moment. God is omnipotent, omniscient and omnipresent - fully present in all moments and in all things, including you. There is no such thing as an insignificant moment. We always have what we need to grow spiritually. Each instant is filled with tremendous opportunity. Everything is in its proper place in the grand scheme of things.

One erroneous belief that must be corrected is the assumption that, by surrender to Divine Will, we will become something different. It is only the ego-self that wishes to be something different. The only reason it wishes to be different is because it views who and what we are now as imperfect. Limiting and negative programs such as depression, anger and anxiety may no longer trouble us. But this doesn't mean we've transformed into something different. It just means there is no longer identification with those tendencies if they arise.

With a subtle shift in perspective, we can begin to accept ourselves as we are and embrace each moment of life as it is. All that is required is to refuse to entertain judgmental thoughts as they arise. To be free of negative programming, it isn't necessary to try and get rid of the judgmental thoughts. Like a stale dish at a buffet line, we simply choose not to indulge in them. What we let go of is our *attachment* to thought processes. Whether the thoughts of themselves continue to arise or not isn't important. By relinquishing attachment to the mind, our relationship with it changes for the better.

How many of us have thoughts, feelings and emotions that we resist or judge as unworthy? How many of us look at a group photo and find ourselves first, complete with all the judgments toward how we appear? How many of us live in constant anxiety? To live in anxiety is to live in fear. *Fear* of not being liked. *Fear* of not being loved or having the approval of others. *Fear* of death. *Fear* of losing our job. *Fear* of not finding our purpose in life. *Fear* of failure. Sometimes turmoil and conflict appears endless. To overcome it can feel like the most daunting of tasks.

One big 'aha!' moment came for me during a period after I had been depressed for a few years. At the time, I was a college student and had transferred to several different colleges and towns. I managed to blame each new town and college for the unhappiness. One day, out of the blue, came the sudden realization that nothing outside myself was causing the feeling of discontent. It became very clear that the reason I was unhappy was due to believing the thoughts that were telling me there was something wrong with my life. Although I didn't fully appreciate it at the time, this was really a profound discovery. There was an addictive attraction to those thoughts, like a strong gravitational pull. That discovery didn't mean instantaneous freedom from the thoughts, although it was certainly the crack in the ego's dam. From that moment, I sought an effective means to be utterly free of the mind and its delusions.

During that time I felt an irresistible draw towards finding spiritual truth, resulting in an intense interest in diverse religions and spiritual practices. This included everything labeled as spiritual – UFO's, channeling, psychics, out-of-body experiences, near-death experiences, past-lives, holistic therapies, etc. The most attractive were the teachings of enlightenment, even though I really had no clue what that was. The teachings of the great saints and mystics, Jesus Christ, Buddha and Ramana Maharshi [3] were huge inspirations. Meditation, prayer and self-enquiry were recommended time and time again. At first I experimented with these on my own as best I could, but I really had no idea whether I was following any of the practices correctly. The fantastic thing about the universe we live in is that when our heart sincerely seeks to move to a more expanded state, the means will be presented to us. Such was my experience. I was pleased to find things were much simpler than I was making them.

Shortly after I first realized my mind was the source of my problems I began a regular practice of meditation. With consistent and confident practice, I began to clearly experience stillness beneath the thoughts. Surprisingly, the mind continued doing exactly what it had done before - the same repetitive stories and depressing thoughts raced through the mind. Not much changed with the content of the

---

[3] As described in the book *Be As You Are – The Teaching of Sri Ramana Maharshi* by David Godman

mind, but I was happy anyway. By maintaining awareness in stillness I found that I could go about the day with no attachment whatsoever to the thoughts floating by. It took perseverance. The attraction to thought is an addiction. As with overcoming any addiction, there can be relapses. As this tendency diminished, the experience of silence became clear. The growing awareness of the Stillness of Divine Presence is described in the section titled 'Advanced Levels of Awareness'

Consciousness

Already existing within everyone is the natural ability to be aware. To be aware is just another way of saying *to notice*. Conscious awareness is forever present whether thoughts are dancing through the mind or not. So awareness really has nothing at all to do with the mind. What is important is that anyone can become aware of the mind. This brings about a whole new way of looking at ourselves. We commonly believe that we *are* the thoughts. When witnessed, thoughts are recognized as objects, appearing as separate from the observer. So, the act of witnessing helps us create some distance from the whole smorgasbord of thoughts.

Conscious awareness is effortless. We can notice the sound of a dog barking down the street while lying on the sofa and can also shift our attention to the raindrops pattering on the rooftop. No conceptual thinking is required to be aware at all. The thought of the rain and the dog actually follows an instant *after* our awareness of them. We notice the sound first, and then there is the labelling of 'dog' and 'raindrops', which comes a split second later. Just this easily, anyone can choose to be aware of the steady stream of thoughts, feelings, emotions and images running through the mind in any moment. Awareness is innately simple. We can simplify terms such as 'meditation', 'consciousness', 'contemplation', 'spirituality', 'enlightenment' and 'surrender' by replacing them with a single word - *awareness*.

Meditation is a means for consciousness to become aware of itself in its pure state. Silence is that which is aware. In fact, it is the only thing that can be aware. It is the eternal 'noticer' of change. The silence itself is the field in which all thought, feeling and emotion arises and subsides. If we imagine fish as symbolic of thoughts, our consciousness is like the water they swim through.

Just as water assumes the form of whatever container it is placed in, consciousness can identify with its boundaries (the mind, body and personality), to the point where it believes that it *is* them. This is like having a clear glass sitting at the bottom of the ocean where water fills the form of the glass but forgets that it is the ocean. When consciousness clings to a thought, it assumes the qualities of the thought. This is like adding food colouring to the water within the glass. The essential nature of the water is the same, only now coloured with a perception of individuality and separation from the rest of the ocean. Thus arises the perceived distinction between the world *as it is* vs. the world *as I experience it*. In this way, the mind is coloured by programming and experiences the universe through the filters of our conditioned perception.

Initially it appears as though there is a 'me' seeking, praying to, worshipping, meditating and attempting to discover a separate 'it' - the 'it', of course, being the presence of Divinity. The 'me' that believes itself separate from Stillness, is the ego-self: the collective identification with the mind, body and personality. It is essentially a bundle of programming that leads us to believe that we exist only as an individual person, who is born, ages, is healthy, sick, happy, sad, wealthy, poor and eventually dies.

Everyone uses the word 'I' countless times every day. 'I' is the reference to 'me'. "*I* thought of that... *I* did this... *I* don't know... *I* am a doctor... *I* am a janitor..." Even if 'I' isn't overtly used, there is still a presumed 'me' that is thought to be the doer of deeds and thinker of thoughts. Following the 'I' comes the illusion of ownership. This is *my* past, *my* car, *my* house, *my* thoughts, *my* beliefs, *my* body. Because there is rarely any conscious experience at all of the true Self, this 'I' of the ego-self is typically the sum total of what a person believes to be "me." The ego-self is made up of form, which is subject to change. The body changes, thoughts and feelings change; the personality has its likes and dislikes, attractions and aversions, beliefs, preferences and opinions, all of which have a beginning and an end.

When we identify only with the mind, body and personality, we do so at the expense of realizing Divine Presence beyond all change, name and form. With increasing awareness of the silence, we become like the wave that begins to realize that there is an infinite ocean of stillness underneath all the perceived changes. We discover that while we may have a mind, body and personality, there is a bigger 'Me' that we haven't been fully conscious of. We realize that we may have a case of mistaken identity - like the sky that forgot its true eternal, formless nature by believing itself to be a cloud.

Duality

Dual means, "Of two; having or composed of two parts or kinds, double, twofold." The entire structure of the ego-self is based on dualistic conditioning which gives rise to the perception of a 'me' and God, good and bad, you and me, this or that, here and there, inner and outer.

Duality is only an appearance. It is a projection of the ego's limits onto the universe. Rather than recognizing the boundless presence of the Absolute, the self lives in a perpetual cloud of multiplicity and separation. It is like the prism that distorts the single, unmoving beam of sunlight into the appearance of several beams, all moving as the prism moves. When duality prevails, so does conflict. As long as identity clings to the mind, body and personality, the world will appear to be filled with chaos.

As long as there is a sense of separation, there will be fertile ground for suffering to flourish. Interestingly enough, duality, separation and suffering only exist within the stories of your mind. It is all just a subtle story that is rehashed on a daily basis. One way to catch the habit in the act is to watch the thoughts flow through the mind. In spite of any attempt to try to stop or control that flow, you may very well find that the steady stream of thoughts continues undaunted. If anything, there tends to be more inner conflict when you try to force the mind in any way.

There is actually nothing inherently wrong with any single one of our thoughts or feelings in reality. It is only a subtle commenting voice that decides there is somehow something wrong with it. A nanosecond after you become aware of this passing thought or feeling, a label is projected onto it. Following the label arises mental commentary that decides whether what is being witnessed is good or bad, desirable or not. The commentary is actually never current, but always of the past. That is why it is rare for anyone to see the world as it is. Instead, for most people, life is often experienced as the popular *Course in Miracles* exercise states, "I only see the past."

The past is continuously being projected onto the present moment and onto everything that we interact with. Suppose the mind is suddenly bombarded with negative thoughts. What would happen if you didn't project any labels onto them? What if you could only be aware of them without assuming that they were good or bad? Without labels, life just is.

As you step away from the identification with the

mind, you step away from duality. As attention is drawn inward, awareness gradually refines to the point where stillness becomes so clear that it can no longer be doubted or ignored. Your True Nature is forever free of duality. Within it, there is no concept of duality or *non*-duality, there is no concept of enlightenment or ignorance, no concept of me or God. It is a profound stillness and fullness without so much as the concept of stillness and fullness.

Advanced Levels of Awareness

As awareness is consistently drawn inward, one gradually opens up to a clear experience of peace. Along the way, profound experiences of joy, love and bliss arise spontaneously and without effort. Regardless of spiritual or religious preferences and cultural backgrounds, many have experienced a moment or moments of sudden expansion at some point in their lives. In some cases, this experience is very brief. Yet, it is not uncommon for the expansion to last for a prolonged period of time (hours, days and even weeks.) These 'peak experiences' are often filled with deep and overwhelming joy, peace and a sense of absolute contentment. Within the peak experience there is nothing seen to be wrong or lacking with life. All is well with everything. Regardless of its duration, such experiences are never forgotten.

Typically, as unexpectedly as it arose, the door to the peak experience closes and one finds that they are back where they were before. It is incredibly rare for one to remain immersed in that expanded condition permanently. After it fades, all that is left is a burning desire to return to that incredible state of aliveness. All else pales in comparison. Seeking the means to reaccess that experience can become an obsession.

These experiences can come about suddenly, without any specific spiritual practice or warning. Typically, there is little understanding of it, let alone any clear idea of how to consciously return to such a state.

Sometimes the opening into great expansion can even bring an initial response of fear. Soon after beginning a regular meditation practice there was a moment where it felt like the bottom dropped out of the experience and a tremendous, unfathomable depth revealed itself. Instantly I was overcome by great fear. I wanted nothing more than to dissolve into that, but at the time there was hesitation. Try as I might, I couldn't shake off the overwhelming fear. After a few moments, that depth seemed to disappear. It would take some time before I was able to release that fear. Years later, I read of a similar description from a great Zen Teacher named Huang Po – *"The substance of the Absolute is inwardly like wood or stone, in that it is motionless, and outwardly like the void, in that it is without bounds or obstructions. It is neither subjective nor objective, has no specific location, is formless, and cannot vanish. Those who hasten toward it dare not enter, fearing to hurtle down through the void with nothing to cling to or stay their fall. So they look to the brink and then retreat."*[4]

Even if you have felt like you have never experienced anything like this or any peak experience, it is of no consequence. The way of awakening begins in this very moment regardless of what the past has been.

There are distinct levels of awareness that become apparent as we open up to Divine presence. These levels represent the opening of awareness to the infinite Silence. We may speak of them as levels, but the growth of consciousness is not so much a linear step-by-step progression as it is a non-linear unfolding. Of itself, the Presence is complete and whole, neither expanding nor contracting. Just as the petals of a flower open to the sunlight, these levels only reflect the degree to which one has opened up to and begun to identify with Silence as the Self.

---

[4] From *'The Zen Teaching of Huang Po: On The Transmission of Mind'* by John Blofeld

Fleeting Awareness of Divine Presence

At this level, the presence of Silence is clear enough to be experienced in any moment. Here it is easy to discern between the ego-self and the Divine Self. This refined level of discernment is known in the ancient Vedic traditions as *viveka*[5]. Without vivika there is little hope for liberation from the confines of ego-identification. At this point, it is easy to discern the changing from unchanging, silence from movement and ego-self from Infinite Self. Any grey-area of doubt or uncertainty becomes very black and white.

Another ancient Vedic term for this is *turiya*, which is a Sanskrit term that means, 'the fourth'. The Silence is experienced as being quite distinct from waking, sleeping and dreaming. It is the permanent background or continuum, which underlies those states. It is like the foundation, the one constant that underlies the daily cycles of day-to-day life. In Zen teachings, the experience of Stillness is known as *satori*. Zen teachings accurately point out that satori is not at all the goal of meditative practice, but rather, just the beginning.

---

[5] *Viveka* is a Sanskrit word that means *'discrimination or distinction'*

In this level, the presence of Silence can be experienced in the midst of any thoughts, feelings or sensations. It is realized to be unconditionally present regardless of the conditions within the body or world. Whether the body is healthy or sick, in the middle of the busiest city or in the calm of an empty cathedral, the silence of Divine presence is evident. But, like the prodigal son, it is only our attention that wanders away from it. It is characteristic of this particular level of awareness that the addiction to the vicissitudes of the mind is still strong enough to draw one's attention out of the field of silence and back into the field of thought. Sometimes this happens more than others. Initially it may be easier to maintain awareness of silence during eyes-closed meditation. While engaging in activity there is often a tendency to lose awareness of it, or forget. The habit of making other things more important is a strong habit to break.

Fortunately, in this state, it is at least clear enough that anytime one remembers, they can choose to become aware again in an instant. Through the continuous practice of repeatedly drawing attention inward, the experience deepens and becomes an ever more attractive option. By consistently prioritizing awareness of the silence above all other options, one soon finds that it becomes possible to remain permanently conscious of it.

A notable characteristic of this level is the growing identification with being the observer/witness of thoughts, feelings and emotions. Prior to this, we thought we *were* those things. Even if inconsistent, at this point there is a clear distinction between subject and object. Therefore the real 'me' is seen to be that which witnesses thought. Thoughts are now seen as objects.

The key aspect of this level is an experiential knowingness that can best be defined as *certainty*. There was a great Teacher from ancient Vedic lore whose Sanskrit name when translated into English meant 'fruit in the palm of the hand'[6]. As bizarre as that sounds, he earned the unique moniker due to the fact that the Infinite had become so clear that the experience for him was as clear as a piece of fruit in the palm of his hand. No doubt remained regarding his true Nature.

Moving Beyond Fleeting Awareness

To move beyond this level into an on going, stable experience of Divine Presence requires consistent prioritization of silence over conceptual thinking. This is like reaching the proverbial fork in the road

---

[6] There is brief reference to this sage in *Shankara's Crest-Jewel of Discrimination* by Christopher Isherwood and Swami Prabhavananda

and having the option present itself in each moment. One must choose which is more important – the mind or peace? Both lead in quite different directions. In addition, there are a few habits that serve as blocks to further advancement of awareness. As these are typically unconscious, simply recognizing them is a significant stage of progress.

Some who begin to experience this level may find that it is not what they expected. Others may find that it is not at all unfamiliar. It is common for many meditators to spend all their time searching past what is already there, to look for something different, seeking something that fits their idea of what Truth is.

Of itself, the presence is so simple that there could be doubt that what is being experienced is really *it*. As long as doubt is left unresolved, there will always be hesitation. Attention will not be given utterly to the stillness as long as doubt dominates. Uncertainty will always keep one feeling separate from the presence and typically lead the ego-self to continue seeking something other than what is here and now.

In the early stages, the experience may not necessarily be filled with mind-blowing bliss and love. It may be just simple, emotionless silence. It may not even seem like an overwhelming presence either. The mind is addicted to change and feels as though something needs to be happening. There is nothing that happens in silence. Boredom can arise in some cases but it is only the ego that can conjure up this idea. To the Infinite Self, each moment is fresh and new.

Bliss, love and great depths of fullness may come and go. Feelings of devotion and inspiration may turn to feelings of flatness. There was a period through which I felt nothing at all. While I certainly wasn't unhappy, there was a belief that I should be experiencing a certain feeling like bliss or love. When we no longer are absorbed in thoughts and feelings as we once were, there is a period of time of adjusting to life without them. Therefore, one great temptation is to cling to a feeling or sensation instead of directing attention to the *source* of the feeling.

I once visited a beach where I stood on a large flat rock on the shoreline watching the waves come and go. When the wave rushed in, the sand and shells would shift and swirl around over the stone and past my feet before being pulled back when the water retreated. The 'rock' of our experience is that which does not come or go. Feelings ebb and flow like the sand and shells. It is of no consequence if they are present or not, we simply maintain awareness on the silent constant beneath them.

Many people have mistaken an expansive feeling of bliss to be the pure experience of the infinite. In such cases, when the high feeling fades, there can be a crash that follows. Amidst the crash is the accompanied feeling that God has abandoned them. It is our inherent innocence that gives all our attention to a feeling, a fleeting experience, instead of the source from which the feeling arose.

A very common trap at this level is to be overly critical of oneself for forgetting to maintain awareness of silence and become absorbed in thinking again. This is best remedied by bringing awareness back in this moment without looking back – not even at what happened a split second ago. The very good news is that the more silence is made a priority, the harder it becomes to ignore it.

Another common trap is to be critical and judge the experience because it is not what we would like it to be. Judging anything we experience is a waste of time. It must be let go of in order to move into greater depths of Self-awareness. Judgmental thoughts can arise but we need not give them any attention. All of these traps come from the core belief that there is a 'me' experiencing an 'it' as if we are looking at infinite stillness from afar. The easiest way to begin to move beyond this level is to begin to diligently surrender <u>all</u>

labels and <u>all</u> commentary with regards to whatever we are experiencing. If we cling to anything the mind says about the experience, we do so at the expense of reinforcing the illusion of separation.

This level of awareness is characterized by the ability to remain consciously aware of Infinite Self in all moments, during meditation and within everyday waking activities. Perpetual awareness is also known in Hindu teachings as *samadhi*. This is where absorption in silence is relatively unbroken. Previously, the number of times throughout the day spent consciously aware of the Self could be counted on one hand; whereas now one could count on one hand the number of moments *not* absorbed in the Self. *The distinction between Fleeting Awareness and Perpetual Awareness exists solely in terms of how much Silence has become a priority.* With each level of growth, it is as if we fly further from the gravitational field of the ego-self. We succumb less to its influence with each advancement in consciousness.

Specific techniques are no longer needed as an aid to access the Stillness. At this point, Silence has become the meditation – being at once the Path, the Teaching, the Teacher, and the Goal. With Perpetual Awareness, a steady depth of bliss, contentment and tranquillity become constant. Each moment feels, and is, complete. This is the beginning of true one-pointedness. In no prior state of consciousness was awareness maintained on any one thing without wavering. Before, attention was easily distracted, constantly drawn into the past and the future. Many teachings speak of 'being in the now'. While there may be value to this concept in terms of applying a practice to reach the awareness of the Self, at this point there is little concern about 'the now' as a concept. One is only concerned with 'the now' via *experience*. Simple, wordless acknowledgment of Stillness is sufficient as the presence of Stillness is the reality of the present moment.

Absorption in silence means there is very little thinking occurring. Even time itself is a mental construct. Therefore, the Presence itself is experienced as a timeless foreverness. While there may be occasional moments when, out of habit, focus drifts outward, these occur less and less frequently. The tendency of habitually drifting out of the Silence and into thinking actually becomes increasingly difficult.

In this state, the outer circumstances of life no longer have the power to disturb inner peace. Whether thoughts continue to flow through the mind or not is unimportant. The attachment and aversion to them has been surrendered to a great extent. Now there is what can be described as an attitude of active indifference. There may certainly be awareness of thought, but there is no real interest in any of them. It is like sitting in your living room with a vague awareness of the traffic passing a block away. One is aware of the passing vehicles, but no interest in them as far as the details of make, model, year and condition are concerned. One is content to rest in the reality of Silence rather than examining illusions.

It may be hard to imagine that there could be more beyond this degree of inner peace but there is always more. Just as Grace drew one toward Divinity, the same impersonal Grace will beckon one further yet. As full and complete as this level seems, one is still subject to dualistic perception. Subtle programming may very well continue to give the impression of separation from Divinity. As awareness is continuously held in Stillness, expansion continues of its own.

Moving Beyond Unbroken Awareness

Residual limiting programs are very much alive and well in this state. If we let go of 90% of it, then it still somehow appears to be 100% in control. Subtle programming continues to operate behind the scenes just beyond our conscious awareness. With advancement of awareness, the ego-self becomes ever more subtle and slick. Some of the proclivities that were found to be quite beneficial in terms of success in the material world have been subsequently applied to spiritual practice – *work hard, try harder, nose to the grind, push yourself, make it happen, personal will-power, nothing worth having comes easily, no pain, no gain.* These attitudes serve us to a certain degree, but we eventually arrive at a place where we cannot advance one iota further in conscious growth by force and control.

Perhaps the main motivation of the ego-self is the whole notion of 'doing to get'. There is still a subject/object relationship with the Stillness at this level of consciousness where the 'me' is forever in the quest to 'do more', 'be more' 'be more surrendered', or 'get deeper' in meditation so that it can 'achieve enlightenment' or 'obtain union with God'. To accomplish it's spiritual goals, the ever valiant 'me' finds ways to 'try harder'. The 'me' wonders why it feels stagnant, why the experience isn't as deep or full or as loving and blissful as it was yesterday. It wonders if it will ever get there, wherever 'there' is.

The ego compares itself with others. When you ask how it's practice is coming along, it is always 'getting there', 'chipping away at it' or 'not where I want to be'. The experience at this level has led the separate 'me' to feel as though it rests in Stillness, like a scuba diver positioned at a certain depth in the ocean. This is precisely where we can identify the fundamental trap at this level. There is a belief that there are two things occurring within us – a 'me' (a *this*) that sinks into Silence (a *that*). This is classic subject/object duality. To be more accurate, there are times when it feels like there are three things - there is the appearance of a 'me' that drifts in some vague area between thoughts and Stillness. Somehow we feel stuck between the two.

So who or what is doing all this doing, floating, trying, failing, and forcing? We have become like a bubble in the ocean. The bubble tries to go deeper and rest in the depths of the ocean. It seeks other enlightened bubbles along the way to help reveal the reality of the great ocean. The bubble is happier some days when it feels like it has grown bigger, and less satisfied when it feels deflated. The bubble compares itself with other bubbles on the quest to find the ocean - after all, some of the bubbles look like they have gone deeper. The bubble exists in time and location. It has a birth and a death, a name and a form. The bubble of 'me' is nothing more than 'my will be done' – the ego's attempt to control.

Anytime we identify with a separate 'me' that does something, we are in error. Surrender to God at greater depth is the all-important key to further growth. Here, we allow the puny 'me' bubble to pop by handing over all our notions of a separate self that is doing-to-get. The only reason we would be so inclined to 'do' at this level is a result of the ego dictating that force will achieve more in the future.

How to let go of this? The ego/mind seems oh so cunning! At this refined state, it is actually quite easy. While attentive of the Silence, also be aware of any label or commentary that comes up with regards to what the current experience is and with regards to who or what 'I am'. Commentary follows labels like smoke follows fire, all that must be done to surrender this is to let go of the labels that are projected onto the experience. There may be labels and commentary following the experience such as 'deep', 'shallow', 'blissful', 'different', 'same', 'too many thoughts', 'good thoughts', 'bad thoughts', 'stagnant', 'flowing'. But what if you didn't cling to anything the mind had to say about the experience?

The bubble of 'me' is created any time we believe the mind's commentary. Labels create a 'this' or a 'that'. Labels and commentary all proceed from a limited perspective. All commentary is essentially the voice of 'my will be done'. By not clinging to labels, commentary will not form. Silence is what remains when attachment to all such mentation is dropped. Indeed, the Way of the Mystic flourishes in a mind utterly freed from conceptual thought processes.

When we feel that any part of our experience or ourselves is not good enough as it is, we aren't giving ourselves completely to *what is*. As such, there is no gratitude for the gifts that permeate our lives. Doing to get is essentially the tendency of looking to a future moment for completion. Meanwhile, we have dismissed what has been given in this moment. We decide that it is incomplete or not good enough. We disregard that Divine Will is presenting exactly what is needed in each moment for growth.

Only the Infinite Self can be aware of the Infinite Self, not something other. Grace has drawn us to this path, not the ego-self. Higher levels of consciousness are simply states where Awareness has become aware of itself in its pure state as permanent peace and fullness. Once it is clear that identification with the ego's commentary is the only obstacle we can choose to surrender it to God in the name of *Thy Will be done O Lord*.

A greater fullness then reveals Itself, to Itself, by

Itself.

Absorption in Divine Presence

"The ocean of Brahman (God) is full of nectar – the joy of the Atman (Infinite Self). The treasure I have found there cannot be described in words, the mind cannot conceive of it. My mind fell like a hailstone into that vast expanse of Brahman's ocean. Touching one drop of it, I melted away and became one with Brahman... This is wonderful indeed!

Here is the ocean of Brahman, full of endless joy. How can I accept or reject anything? Is there anything apart or distinct from Brahman? Now, finally and clearly, I know that I am the Atman, whose nature is eternal joy. I see nothing. I hear nothing. I know nothing that is separate from me."[7]

The Silence is experienced as being beyond all traces of objectivity, conflict, or change. It is full and complete, lacking nothing. When identified with the Stillness of the Self, there is no longer any interest in the mind's labels and commentary at all whatsoever. Dualistic concepts of 'enlightened' or 'not enlightened' or 'Divine Union' have all become

---

[7] Adi Shankaracharya quote borrowed from *'The Crest Jewel of Discrimination – Viveka-Chudamani'* by Christopher Isherwood and Swami Prabhavananda

meaningless. For lack of a better way of describing it, one really becomes absorbed in that which they give their full attention to. By repeatedly drawing attention into the silence this is the case. One becomes utterly absorbed in its unspeakable presence.

Previously, certain thoughts had a certain charge to them. A 'poor me' story would have a lot of sad, depressed energy associated with it, for example. Now, if the exact same thought floated through, there would be no attachment to it. All thoughts that once had energy are now experienced as hollow and lifeless – if they even arise at all. Relationship with thought is like the relationship of space with a shooting star. The thought comes and goes in a blink, but infinite space is unmoved. Divine Union is nothing more than abiding *as* the Infinite Silence. This is the 'Kingdom of Heaven'. It is the same presence that has been experienced by any true sage or mystic that has ever lived.

The leap from Fleeting Awareness to Divine Union is not really that big. After all, where is there to go? All that needs be done is to simply acknowledge the presence of Silence, and refuse to cling to something *other* than that. This takes great commitment and willingness. While consciousness itself is pure simplicity, we have a lifetime, or *lifetimes*, of

investment in the ego-mind as being the true Self.
That is quite a strong gravitational field to escape
from. Therefore, patience and persistence are key
virtues to live by.

All these levels of awareness, from Fleeting
Awareness to Union, represent the growing
relationship with the exact same Silence. At sunrise
we may have our curtains open a crack or all the way.
The sun is not the least bit concerned either way.
Whether we live in darkness or not is our choice.
Ordinarily, it is presumed that our well-being is
caused by something external. It becomes very
evident that only mental programming causes
suffering, while bliss, peace, love and joy have no
cause.

A major obstacle that may very well keep one from
experiencing this level of awareness are beliefs in
worthiness. If we don't feel worthy of God's grace, or
of being in a state of permanent joy, then guess what?
We will find that state is forever beyond our reach.
Compassion is a by-product of growing awareness.
Yet, paradoxically, it can be a means for growth as
well. Compassion is mastered by unconditional
acceptance. Acceptance comes when we surrender
attachment to all commentary, as mentioned earlier.
Freedom from the fetters of the ego does not come

as long as we continue to hold onto resentments or judgements toward others or ourselves. Only the ego-self and its commentary judges, deems that we are not worthy, and holds onto resentments from the past.

A subtle trap that often goes unnoticed is where surrender itself becomes a mechanism of manipulating God. In other words – 'If I surrender this, then God will give me what I want'. By this slight of hand, the ego, a.k.a. *my will be done* cloaks itself in the nobility of *Thy Will be done*. To remedy this, we must let go of attachments to an outcome. That is, let go of 'what I want to happen' and assume that God has a better plan than we do. How do we tell if ego is in control? Because the pure experience of Silence and joy are always clouded over when *my will* is engaged. It is believed that they will result from conditions and circumstances. *My will* = anxiety and stress. *Thy will be done* is at its purest when all 'I want's' are relinquished. The Stillness of Divine Presence simply must be more important than the ego-self's agenda. *Thy Will be done* is not a practice that seeks an end result in the future. Instead, it equals instant peace. It is its very own reward. If it doesn't appear this way, the ego-mind is stubbornly clinging to an investment in an outcome.

QUESTION AND ANSWER

Can one fall from higher states of consciousness or do they remain permanent?

It has been my experience that potential distractions can be present at virtually every step of the way. As this is a narrow path, there is no room for deviation or wavering from the experience of Peace. It is not possible to be in control and free at the same time. All effort to try and control what freedom will look like or attempt to modify it or bend the path toward *my will* only serves as a delay to freedom.

An intense and unwavering devotion to God opens one up to Divine Grace. It is ultimately only via grace that our Higher Self can be realized. Yet this is not by any means a passive pathway. A practice that involves letting go of positions is a very pro-active endeavour. Continuous attentiveness and devotion to a powerful spiritual practice is the best way to ensure that an advanced state of Awareness won't be prone to compromise.

I find it hard to accept the idea of surrender to God. It seems very religious. Horrible things have been done throughout history in the name of devotion to God. How can I reconcile this?

All horrible things done in God's name only come from ignorance of God's true nature. It is important to look at all the notions that we have been conditioned with regarding God. Strive for experience, not concepts. If the word 'God' is upsetting, use another word in its place. When we speak of surrender *this does not mean surrender to a concept of God.*

It is easy to look out into the world at current events or into the past and see the staggering amount of suffering that has occurred. The Peace spoken of in this writing does not refer to the peace of everyone on the planet getting along. That is an unrealistic social experiment. True Peace is an unconditional *presence*. It prevails in spite of what is happening in the world around us. And the experience of this Presence is far greater than the greatest thing the mind could conceive of.

By simply abiding as that presence, all of mankind is positively impacted in the most profound way

What is the difference between the will of God and personal will power?

There is no shortage of information available out there on how to effectively channel, tap into, develop and apply personal willpower. This involves creating, attracting or manifesting the life that *I want. I want* is the core of the ego/self.

The 'laws of manifestation', as they are often called, do work and one can and does attract to them what is held in mind. This is already occurring for everyone even though it is mostly unconscious. The desire for a better life is not so much the issue as is the attachment to the belief that happiness can only come in a certain way, shape or form.

A significant leap in consciousness occurs when victimhood is relinquished and accountability begins to take its place. The enhancement of personal will serves a great purpose by opening us to a more empowered state of being. Now, one can actively begin to make changes from within. Attempting to rearrange the outside world without changing how we hold it in mind is as ineffective as trying to comb your hair on the mirror instead of on your head!

The laws of manifestation are impressive, productive

and empowering and may very well lead to a great deal of material success, but due to the built-in limitations of *my will*, personal willpower will forever fail to lead to the discovery of Silence of the Self.

So, does this mean we don't apply the laws of manifestation? I do not think it can be avoided. But, we must recognize what the intention behind a given desire is. Are we attached to the outcome? Do we feel that we cannot be happy unless we obtain a certain object? Is your joy totally dependent upon the conditions of a certain outcome? Could you still be happy if you *don't* get your way?

To align with Divine Will involves letting go of the attachment to the outcomes and limiting agendas of the ego's personal will. Very little material on personal will power teaches how to effectively turn personal will over to Divine Will. What profit is really gained by manifesting all the wealth in the world only to arrive at the moment of death with no conscious awareness of the Source of *true* Power?

A practical approach in aligning with the Will of God is to not suppress the desires of the self, but to understand them. One can very well expect numerous desires to arise along the way. Personal will clings to desire and tries to force its hand in order to get its way. There is priceless wisdom in recognizing that God always has a better plan. My favorite quote is actually one I found on a refrigerator magnet –

"Good morning, this is God. I will be handling all of your problems today. I will not need your help. Have a great day!"

Desires are not bad or wrong, but often misplaced. The ego perceives lack and believes that the objects of the world are the source of its happiness. Because the objects of the world are as fleeting as the clouds in the sky, the best they can provide is temporary pleasure. Like the three year old, the ego often wants what it doesn't have and has what it doesn't want. It is relentless in its persistence that there is something lacking or missing. As one desire is fulfilled, another arises in its place. Our assumed source of happiness is then projected onto the next relationship, the next job, the next house, etc. I have met so many people that have so much in terms of material possessions who aren't content at all.

The notion of surrender to God sounds very passive.

There is nothing as engaging and alive as the practice of active surrender. This requires a continuous commitment, devotion, attentiveness and willingness. Many people have ended up in a detached state of aloofness, stagnancy and flatness due to misunderstanding of this key teaching. Ultimately all that is really surrendered is the *attachment and identification* with the ego-self and all its thoughts, desires, fears and anxieties. It is possible for all these things to still arise in our awareness just as they always have, and yet to be totally free from them at the same time.

When the experience of the Stillness becomes clear, so does the understanding that in any given moment, attention is either given to thoughts or to Stillness. It becomes apparent that to cling to conceptual thinking is to re-enter the domain of the mind and all the conflict that it brings. Ultimately, immersion in Silence requires one to surrender nothing more than the attraction to thinking. While it may not appear this way at first, the truth is, there is nothing simpler.

I have heard of those who awakened suddenly. Some without adhering to any particular spiritual practice. It was like somewhere along the way, the lights came on.

Such cases are incredibly rare. You are probably a thousand times more likely to be struck by lightning than to wake up without any effort or guidance at all.

Is it necessary to surrender everything?

The only thing that is really ever surrendered is the tendency to mistake illusion for reality. Surrender is a moment-by-moment decision that can be likened to mud settling and leaving the water clear. Like our true Essence, the water was present all along but only obscured by deeply ingrained programming. By withdrawing all attachments to illusions only the pure reality of the Self alone remains.

The notion of surrendering might sound a bit ominous to the ego-self. But surrender is really nothing more than pure simplicity. There is nothing complicated about it as long as we have a clear understanding of *how* to put it into practice. We may just as well replace the word 'surrender' with 'letting go', 'allowing' and an attitude of 'what will be will be'.

To drop attachment is to relinquish ownership. We tend to think ownership involves only material objects, but here we refer more to the ownership of concepts, beliefs and ideas. The only place ownership can exist is within our thoughts. It is not necessary to own so much as a single thought. Ownership means that, instead of a thought being merely *a* thought, it becomes *my* thought – *my* story, *my* beliefs, *my* idea.

The programs through which we view the world and many of our cherished beliefs were never really ours to begin with. Many of them were picked up from our upbringing. These may include religious and political preferences and prevailing positive or negative attitudes.

In the highest sense, nobody really owns anything. It is more accurate to say that all that you now have is on temporary loan from the Universe – this includes your body and thoughts. Everything already belongs to God. Surrendering is only acknowledging rightful ownership.

Is renunciation the same as surrender? Is it necessary to leave everything including my family, job, loved ones, and possessions?

True renunciation involves giving up illusions not life. It isn't the mind and the world around that changes but, rather, how you *relate* to them. All that needs to ever be renounced is the identification with the mind. Aside from that, whether you have material possessions or not is really not important. You need not try and change anything in your life as it is right now. Not even the thoughts that race through your head.

I know it is the ego that is the problem, but I can't seem to get rid of it.

Drop the idea that you need to get rid of it.

Any quest to slay, destroy or kill the ego only serves to reinforce its dominance. This puts a 'me' against the ego - a noble form of duality, but a limitation nonetheless. The hidden presumption here is that something is wrong (judgment) and needs to change ("I can only be free if I change these thoughts or feelings.") Attempts to control the ego and its thoughts will always be *counter*-productive.

When I first began to meditate, rather than peace, the practice resulted in more headaches than relaxation. I had assumed that if my mind wasn't still, I wasn't doing it correctly. This is one of the most common misconceptions regarding meditation. For the longest time, I was resisting everything that arose in my awareness instead of letting it be.

With an effective practice of meditation, contemplation, centering prayer, or affirmation, the relentless addiction to thinking can be overcome. Through persistence, the tendency to fade into thought streams lessens and one becomes more the observer rather than the participant in the mind's activity. At first, this is often easier during a sitting, eyes closed practice of meditation. With on-going dedication to our practice the ability to remain a witness to thoughts can be maintained in the midst of physical activity.

Eventually, one is able to rest in inner Stillness no matter what is happening in the mind or world around. At this point we become the eye of the storm, so to speak. As awareness is absorbed in Silence, the addiction to the mind gradually dissolves of its own. Silence eventually becomes the meditation. Even the mind itself may eventually still of its own accord. But, there is no longer any personal investment left with regards to whether the mind ever stills or not.

Is the experience of Stillness the same thing that has been described as the Void?

As the experience deepens and solidifies, it is experienced as profound fullness, bliss, love, silence, peace and joy. Bliss and love may grow and fade in intensity, yet the Silence remains. Strangely enough, even if an experience of bliss comes and goes, it is thoroughly enjoyed when present and not missed when absent. Silence fills all sense of lack. 'Void' is not how I typically describe the experience. But it makes sense why it would be a descriptive term as the Silence is void of form. Once cannot capture Silence with words and thoughts any more than a deep experience of love can be explained adequately.

I have a strong desire to know God, but I am afraid of losing control.

Only the ego fears loss. Even though it feels real and feels like the real me, it never is. Contrary to what the ego tends to believe, life only improves without it. The fact is the ego never was in control. Believing it was 'me' and that 'I' was in control, turned out to be the very source of all that was ever unpleasant, unfulfilling and painful in life. For fun, I had the idea of titling this book, "All is Well When Nobody Shows Up."

While fear can be common at first along this path, it is also transitory. Unlike the Infinite Self, the limited self, along with its fears, has a lifespan. The joy of discovering Divinity is so great that it is worth everything to walk through fear, no matter how intense or real it may seem. To turn away because of fear will lead to a life that may very well be comfortable and predictable, but not necessarily liberating.

Many people are resistant to change. Even if the doorway to something greater presents itself, they often pass on the opportunity due to fear, uncertainty and the comfort of clinging to familiar boundaries, even if they result in dissatisfaction and inner pain.

Does the ego-self need to die in order to realize the Self?

By bringing attention inward consistently, what is real will stay, and what is not will fall away. What dies is the tendency to believe that you are something that is born, changes, suffers and dies. Even so, this death can be likened to when we dream and wake up. You could say the dream dies when you wake up, but it is more accurate to say that it never was real to begin with.

What are some useful qualities that may benefit a spiritual student?

Dedication

Jesus taught us the Great Commandment - *"You shall love the Lord your God with all your heart, and with all your soul, and with all your mind."*[8] By following this Great Teaching, all that is needed will reveal itself in each

---

[8] Lamsa Bible Matthew 22:37

moment.[9] All of creation, seen and unseen unconditionally serves and assists all who desire spiritual Truth. Especially if the desire to know God outshines all other desires.

In my experience, the pull to experience God was not an intellectual curiosity. Rather, there was a deep and impersonal draw toward it that I couldn't resist despite my best effort at times! I struggled with the fact that this is not a common life pursuit in society as a whole. It was hard to relate to those who did not share the same interest.

Initially it felt like there was a 'me' that chose to be spiritual. Now, I don't believe this to be the case for anyone. All who seek to know God are pulled toward it. Perhaps this can be considered spiritual ripeness. Even so, one must still pro-actively direct awareness toward the Silence. The Reality of the Presence of God is discovered in the Infinite Silence.

Through commitment, the pathway to the goal is hastened. Along with desire, wise and effective use of time is also imperative for progress. The greatest impediment to progress, in any area of concern, is lack of commitment.

---

[9] As the popular saying goes… *"When the student is ready, the teacher will appear"*

Clarity

Without any clear sense of direction, one could easily remain lost in a sea of uncertainty. Finding a clear practice can save huge amounts of time and money. This must involve learning what is of value and what is best avoided. From the base of the mountain it may appear as though there are a multitude of paths to the summit. Many of them gradually weave and wind their way around the mountain through all the valleys, caves, streams and forests. The quickest path to the summit cautiously sidesteps the various diversions and makes efficient use of time and resources. As with any unfamiliar territory, a valid map or guide who is intimately familiar with the terrain is of immense importance. The purpose of a book such as this is to provide at least a beginning guide that can narrow one toward the goal by helping cultivate spiritual discernment.

In terms of freedom from the mind's house of mirrors, clear guidance is invaluable. To go at it alone is the equivalent to walking blindfolded through a minefield. The habits of the mind are subtle in the extreme and the entanglement within its programs is deep and relentless. A valid guide is one that has walked the path and is familiar with all the subtleties of experience and who is identified with the Divine

Self as the sole Reality of all that is.

From one perspective there appears to be virtually endless pathways to God, though when it comes down to it, there is really only one. All pathways will eventually bring one to the point where Stillness must be chosen over the mind and its endless conundrums. Present moment awareness is the only way in which the fetters of ignorance can be transcended. While the paths to the top of the mountain appear numerous, at some point all must take the same final step to ascend the summit.

I have met several people over the years that claim to receive guidance from presumed spiritual gurus (both alive and deceased), whom they had never personally met. It is questionable whether or not some of these teachers are authentic or just parroting spiritual concepts. Some look impressive, but do not live what they teach. Some are indeed the real deal. In either case, one can place a stick of incense in front of their picture or figurine and call them 'Guru' or 'Master' if they want. But, at the end of the day, it is you that must do the work by applying the teaching in your life. Even the greatest sage, mystic or saint cannot do it for you.

Some presumed guides include astral entities,

'ascended masters', angels, as well as channelled information presumably from famous sages and saints. Some claim to receive guidance in dreams, visions or hearing voices. This form of guidance is not recommended. In the vast majority of cases I have seen, the guidance is either coming from the subtleties of the students very own ego, or a source on the 'other side' that is only *presumed* to be competent. Just because it is in etheric form doesn't automatically qualify it as being saintly. One is not an 'ascended master' by virtue of the fact that they have declared themselves as such. Any true Master, whether in a body or not, will tell you the same thing. Even if rarely followed, all that is needed is available in this world. When in doubt, just read over the first Great Commandment of Jesus Christ again.

Dreams are a very unreliable source of instruction. Oftentimes, visions and voices are nothing more than elaborate and fanciful imaginings that only appear legitimate. The tricky thing is that from the surface of the mind it is almost impossible to know if a vision is valid or not. The odds are overwhelmingly against these forms of guidance as being sufficient for spiritual progress.

True guidance has appeared on this planet over the years through the great sages, saints and mystics. The purest channels for Divinity always point back toward the heart of the student. Your heart is where the Silence of Divine Presence may be discovered. It is indeed closer than your next breath.

Humility

When humility is lacking, growth draws to a halt. There is a clear-cut difference between "I know that already" vs. a silent openness and willingness to let go of presumed intellectual understanding. To be aware of the mind's limited nature is to be automatically humbled.

Within addiction recovery programs no lasting recovery is likely to happen without self-honesty. Without the humility required to be totally honest about one's shortcomings, it is not possible to make it past the very first of the 12 steps. *It is not possible to recover from any addiction without humility – most certainly not even the addiction to the ego-self.*

The positions of the ego create a mask that we unknowingly wear until we wind up believing the mask to be an authentic representation of our true self. Among other things, the masks of the self set one apart in some way: either to make one greater than or more special than another, or less significant and less worthy.

Without humility not only are we unable to see ourselves clearly, but the actual essence of Divinity can never be clear either. It is possible to be very self-centered, and yet still believe one is generous. It is possible to be a chronic drug-abuser but still believe we are in control. It is possible to be caught in illusion, and still think that spiritual clarity has been attained. A key part of the 12-Step recovery programs is to be willing to take a 'fearless moral inventory'. This is absolutely necessary for any true spiritual practice such as this.

The ego tends to rely on its own strength rather than seeking help. Oftentimes, being right becomes more important than being free. At its core the ego does nothing more than subtly reject God in favor of it's own agenda. Even the slightest shred of openness is enough to begin to signal the beginning of the end of its dominance. By opening the curtain just a tiny bit, the room is filled with sunlight.

The very structure of the ego was set in place as a result of past experience and the conditioning of society being etched into the innocent mind. Curiously, attachment to this conditioning can come to an end with the help of innocence within a meditative practice. Nevertheless, it is important to be aware of the potential pros and cons of innocence.

The Perils and Advantages of Innocence

Humility and innocence often go hand in hand. However, the truly humble need not be naïve. Naïve innocence has the tendency to be attracted to virtually anything that is labelled as 'spiritual'. As a result, one can be drawn to paths that are deterrents to growth. Countless teachings, practices and material are found to exist under the title 'spirituality' that are anything but.

Naïve innocence tends to take things at face value. It will wander though a new-age fair and visit every single booth, psychic and card reader. It will start at one end of the bookshelf on spirituality and read down the line believing most of the information to be of value. It will assume that because something was presented in a book or on TV, then it must be valid. When looking for spiritual teachers, it may mistake popularity for an automatic sign of legitimacy. Naïve innocence prevails in those who have not been educated properly or had enough experience to develop mature discernment. There have been reports of people mauled to death trying to feed wild grizzly bears by hand. Just because it looks big and cuddly doesn't mean it won't kill you! Sometimes, there is a big difference between how things *appear* and how things *are*. The fact of the matter is, nearly all spiritual seekers go through this phase to varying degrees.

Refined spiritual discernment develops in time through experience and proper education. Eventually and ideally, one may remain humble, but is no longer naïve. This is probably best defined as *wisdom*. Here the big, cuddly looking grizzly can be appreciated from a safe distance. The wise and humble are very aware of what is out there, but time is not wasted on distractions. Appearances no longer deceive as long as essence is recognized. Diversions are avoided, not from fear so much as choosing for efficient use of time. The first step to the development of wisdom, is finding a suitable practice one can place confidence in and which can be applied continuously.

As one begins the inner journey of Self-realization, wisdom involves letting go of the attraction to side-paths as well as all ideas of what God is. One quote that has remained with me from my Catholic upbringing is "The eye has not seen and the ear has not heard and the heart of man has not conceived the things which God has prepared for those who love him."[10] God cannot be grasped with the senses or the mind. And yet, while conceptual knowledge is an obstacle in the early stages, it can be useful. The

---

[10] 1 Corinthians 2:9 Lamsa Bible

intellect needs to be satisfied and educated to a certain extent. Legitimate spiritual teachings and material help cultivate greater awareness and understanding. The purpose of satisfying the intellect is to remove doubt and inspire. The result is greater confidence in your practice.

Willingness

Willingness means applying the spiritual principles you have been taught with consistency. One could read all about health and fitness but never commit to a regimen. All the knowledge in the world *about* fitness doesn't help one become fit. What is required is to put what is learned into practice and do the work.

Willingness cannot be mentioned without addressing forgiveness. If there were a slogan for forgiveness, it would read 'Forgiveness – there is no freedom without it'. The wonderful book, A Course In Miracles has great wisdom on forgiveness[11]. By looking at the things you may be unwilling to forgive, you can also see a story supporting them, justifying whatever position is being held. This is how to recognize an attachment.

---

[11] see lesson in A Course In Miracles Workbook titled 'What Is Forgiveness?'

An unwillingness to forgive means that one is clinging to stories from the past along with their associated conflicting emotions. Without willingness to forgive, there can be no lasting inner peace and joy. Maybe a glimpse here and there at best, but nothing permanent. One can only grow so far while holding on to grievances, then a point is reached where a choice must be made to either hold on to it or let it go.

Initially, the very term forgiveness may be associated with resentment toward others, but we must also be willing to forgive ourselves if we wish to experience peace. All justified resentments are only mental rationalizations that maintain suffering in some form.[12]

Gratitude

There can be no freedom without *gratitude*. Those who are perpetually angry, pessimistic and constantly critical are not spending much time acknowledging what they are grateful for. The consistently grateful are the consistently happy. Gratitude is such a simple

---

[12] "Holding on to anger is like grasping a hot coal with the intent of throwing it at someone else; you are the one who gets burned." Buddha

choice and results in immense transformational power. In addition to dissolving victim mentality, gratitude also erases guilt, shame, judgment and fear. It is much more enlivening to find something to be grateful for than finding something to condemn. It is up to us to decide how we choose to view our lives.

PART II

THE WAY

Insights on Devotion

Popular methods of spiritual devotion often involve practices of contemplation and meditation. Most forms of meditation are practiced while sitting with eyes closed, whereas contemplation is more of an on-going, moment-by-moment dedication to a particular inspirational teaching that is held in mind throughout the day.

The technique presented in the following pages is a combination of both meditation *and* contemplation. This particular method offers a simple means to direct attention inward in all moments with the help of a very powerful phrase. It can be applied with eyes open anytime throughout the day, and it can also be practiced with eyes closed as is common with traditional meditative practices.

Many people struggle with their practice of meditation due to mistaken beliefs. Simply hearing the word 'meditation' can evoke a host of connotations regarding what it allegedly involves. Rigid postures, repetitive chants, strict diets, burning incense, guru worship and strenuous concentration are all commonly believed to be necessary ingredients to successful practice. Yet, all too often, one's assumptions weave an unnecessary web of complexity. It is much simpler than commonly believed.

Awareness is perhaps a better word to use, as that is what meditation enlivens within us. There is only one way to move beyond the identification with the ego-self, and that is via *present moment awareness*. It is redundant to say 'present moment awareness' as awareness can *only* occur in the present. There is no rule stating that any technique at all is required in order to enliven awareness. But due to the strong addiction to the ego-mind, a clear and confident practice may prove to be vital.

This particular meditation technique can be used successfully by anyone with ease. When applied consistently it is effective regardless of the circumstances of mind or body or what is happening around you. It will even work whether you believe it will or not.

The technique helps with the following:

    1. Enlivens present moment awareness.

2. Assists one in moving beyond the addiction to thought and emotion.

3. Draws awareness into Silence.

4. Helps one overcome the relentless influence of negative thought processes.

5. Enhances spiritual devotion to the Higher Power/Creator by whatever name one would choose to call it.

6. Cultures awareness of unconditional peace, joy and love.

Proper instruction can quickly clarify what could otherwise amount to *years* of trial and error. When I began meditating, I had a constant lingering doubt with respect to whether or not I was doing it correctly. This is quite common. Unfortunately, peace will never be found where doubt prevails. In the name of clarity, all the basic steps for this practice have been presented.

Some may disagree with presenting meditation instruction in a book. The argument is that live teaching is always the better alternative. Of course, live instruction is preferable *when available*.[13] However,

---

[13] And when competent.

one would be remiss to make no effort at all to share a teaching like this in a book due to the simple fact that live teaching isn't always so readily available.

If Divine providence deems it necessary for you to have live instruction, so be it. If Divine providence has placed this book in your path, so be it. The desire for spiritual advancement isn't 'your' desire so much as a mysterious, impersonal pull. The same Force that brought you into the world is the same Force that has sustained you up to this point in time. It is the exact same Force that now stirs interest in this information. It is the Grace of the Force alone that surrounds you in each moment and presents exactly what is needed for growth.

Many may feel a great amount of devotion to Divinity and still question how to direct one's efforts most effectively in order to enhance its presence in their lives. Some may find their current spiritual practice is too complex or ineffective. Many find that subtle doubts prevail in spite of one's best efforts. In terms of practice, complexity only leads to further complexity and doubt never results in significant progress. A clear and direct teaching that can be practiced consistently and with confidence will move mountains.

THE TECHNIQUE

The technique itself is presented in three parts. 1. The wording of the technique 2. The explanation of the Star Word and 3. Point of Awareness. The steps on how to use it will be addressed following these.

The meditation technique is as follows…

1. Glory To ★ In the Highest

Anytime you think **Glory To ★ In The Highest**, do so simply, naturally and effortlessly. Just as effortlessly as you read these words. It should be as simple as any other thought. There must be no force or strain involved at all whatsoever. More instruction will be given on how to use this in the following pages.

This phrase is powerful because it represents the very essence of devotion itself. Acknowledgement of Divinity is something can be utterly absent from day-to-day life. With the help of this technique, it can be made a priority. This phrase is one of the most powerful things anyone can think.

For reference, this phrase comes from the New Testament - Luke 2:14. It is more commonly known in its Latin form as *Gloria in Excelsis Deo*. The Latin version may be used as the technique, but it may come at the expense of the **Star Word** and the potential benefit it brings.

2. The Star Word

This technique is more commonly known in English as *Glory to God in the Highest*. Though not everyone may feel comfortable using the word 'God'. Instead, this technique utilizes what is known as a 'Star Word' in place of the word 'God'. This is where you replace the '★' with *your concept of the greatest force for good in the universe. In addition, the word you select must have no negative connotations associated with it.*

If the word 'God' is wholly positive and is your personal concept for the greatest force for good in the universe, then it is your ideal Star Word. But if it contains negative connotations, take some time to think of what other word comes up for you instead.

Examples for the Star Word are potentially endless. Common ones may include - 'Allah', 'Great Spirit', 'Brahman', 'Love', 'Infinite Silence', 'Christ', 'Grace' 'Divinity', 'Peace', 'Buddha', 'Krishna', 'Holy Spirit', 'Joy', 'Peace', 'Harmony', etc. It is best to keep the Star Word short and simple.

There are also many not so common Star Words that I have heard of over the years. Once, a young woman who was attending a weekend retreat in Australia chose the word 'purple' for her Star Word. When I asked her why, she described a near death experience where she suddenly found herself surrounded by a 'purple mist'. The purple mist was filled with such overwhelming peace, love and perfection that it was totally transformational for her. She also described how her long deceased grandmother greeted her there, looking more vibrant and happy than she ever remembered. Her concept for Divinity was therefore not 'God' and all the ideas she had been conditioned with, but simply 'purple' and what it represented to her.

Some who struggle with finding a Star Word may simply pick what it is they want most in their life. In this case words like Peace, Love or Happiness can be chosen. When I first learned to meditate I only wanted to be happy and content with who I was and what I was faced with in my life. So, at the time, I picked 'peace' as my Star Word since that is what symbolized the greatest force for good with no negative connotations to me.

To find what feels right to you, simply sit, close your eyes and begin thinking the phrase with whatever word comes to mind first. You may find that the word that fits for you will come up quite naturally. Do not stress over it. Take your time and be gentle with each and every step of this practice.

The Star Word is the only part of this technique that can be changed if needed. Perhaps in time your concept may change. It doesn't have to, but it might. In that case your word may change and evolve as you do. The rest of the phrase is just fine as it is and is better left alone.

Should you feel a change is in order, just keep the key criteria in mind - *The word you select must <u>always</u> represent your concept for the greatest Force for good in the universe with no negative connotations.*

3. The Awareness Point

Each time you think Glory to ★ In The Highest, gently place attention in your heart. This should be done simply. It must never be any more difficult than thinking of your big toe, for example. Due to the fact that there is a deep tendency to project Divinity outside of us, placing attention in the heart each time you think the technique will help dissolve such subconscious tendencies. Divinity, by whatever name anyone would chose to call it, is ultimately discovered in the heart, the very core of our being.

The Five Steps to Tranquility

1. Notice the mind.
2. Think the technique.
3. Let it go.
4. Allow whatever happens to happen.
5. Repeat.

1. Notice the mind.

Gently be aware of the thoughts, images and emotions floating through the mind, as well as the sensations in the body. It doesn't matter what the mind is doing or what we are feeling, we simply take a brief instant to notice.

2. Think the Technique.

Think **Glory to ★ in the Highest** just as you would think any other thought. You do not need to create a certain mood or feeling to go with it. Whatever feeling arises naturally is OK. Simply think the technique in the midst of whatever you happen to be thinking or feeling.

3. Let it go.

We don't try and hold onto the technique or maintain unwavering focus on it. Nor do we think it over and over in rapid succession while trying to block out other thoughts. There is no straining or trying involved with this practice at all whatsoever. We simply think the technique and let it go.

4. Allow whatever happens to happen.

Either you are allowing or controlling. *Allowing* leads to peace, *controlling* leads to something other than peace. Whatever the experience is when you think **Glory to ★ in the Highest** allow it be exactly as it is.

5. Repeat.

Gently bring attention back to Step 1. You may become aware at this point that *noticing* has already effortlessly begun the moment you remember to return to the technique.

Pointers

❖ For Step 1 a brief moment is all that is needed to notice whatever is moving through the mind and whatever you are feeling in the body before going to Step 2.

❖ It is most powerful to think this technique inwardly. It is not necessary to chant, sing or speak it aloud.

❖ We never need to feel a certain way while using the technique. This practice will work as long as we do it. It will be effective regardless of the state of the mind or body. It is powerful in spite of whatever mood we may be in.

❖ Whatever happens naturally with this practice is ok. During meditation, we <u>never</u> try and force the experience to be a certain way.

❖ Only 'my will' of the ego is unwilling to allow whatever happens to happen. It chooses to try and control the experience.

❖ Anytime there is difficulty with your practice,

simply look to see which of the Five Steps you are not doing or are having problems with.

Eyes Open Practice

Using this practice with eyes open is simple - just think **Glory to ★ in the Highest** and then let it go. This should not distract you from whatever you are doing. After all, it is no more difficult than thinking any other thought.

Eyes open practice can be easily forgotten, especially when this practice is new. Most are habitually drawn outward on thought with incredible ease. Each of our experiences has the potential to trigger a set of thought processes that draw attention into the past or future. With practice, one will find it is easier to maintain awareness in the present throughout the day. Gradually such thought processes may even begin to lose their appeal. By using the technique with attention in the heart, you may find that your attention remains there effortlessly for longer and longer periods.

When dealing with stressful situations, eyes open practice is a phenomenal tool to have. Rather than becoming completely absorbed in stressful thoughts and feelings, simply apply the technique and it will help to replace tension with calmness.

Eyes Closed Practice

Ideally, time should be set aside for eyes closed practice each day to go with eyes open practice. As a general guideline about twenty minutes two to three times a day is recommended - once in the morning before you start your day, then again in the late afternoon after work and then when you go to bed at the end of the day. It is great to use the technique until you fall asleep. Of course there are no fixed rules about this. Everyone will fit the practice into his or her own unique schedule and lifestyle.

It is very rewarding to create a routine where you take time to close your eyes and ease into this practice. The rest that comes from eyes closed practice is deep and relaxing. One can experience greater depths of peace and stillness than may be experienced with eyes open. Each experience of the stillness with eyes closed means there is more likelihood of that experience becoming clear with eyes open throughout the day.

If sleep is hard to come by at night, the technique may be used eyes closed instead. The rest that results may even be deep enough that you feel rested in spite of a sleepless night.

When the practice is new, it is a good idea to minimize distractions when meditating with your eyes closed. Turn off the music, television; silence your phone to help minimize distractions. Take some time to turn your senses inward and just be with yourself. It is worth it.

Aside from being able to use the technique eyes open, what other ways does this practice differ from other meditation practices?

The notion of meditation commonly evokes images of rigid uncomfortable postures and strenuous inward focus. It is commonly assumed that we need to forcibly stop or exert some sort of control over the stream of thoughts in order to achieve a state of inner peace. If meditation is meant to bring about peace and relaxation it must be simple, not an exercise in strain and complexity.

If there is a belief that your mind must be different than what it is in any given moment, then chances are ripe that you will fall into the ineffective trap of applying force to control it.

Therefore one key difference between this practice and traditional forms of meditation is that this method does not involve mind control. It isn't the mind that changes so much with regular practice but our *relationship* with the mind. Thoughts don't actually need to change regardless of their quantity or quality.

In addition, there are no specific diets, postures, music, chants or belief systems required. There is no need to alter your current beliefs. It isn't even necessary to believe that the practice will work in order to benefit from it.

QUESTION AND ANSWER

Even though this practice is simple, the mind may very well find ways to complicate it. Forcefulness can sneak into the practice and turn what should be the simplest thing into a tiresome chore.

As long as the basics are clear, then we need only follow the fundamental steps in order for the practice to be effective. The power in this approach forever lies in its profound simplicity. **Glory to ★ in the Highest** applied via The Five Steps is really all that is needed. Aside from that, the rest of this book is generous commentary.

What is the best advice for beginners?

We can only work with who and what we are right now. Accept that wherever you are and whatever you are experiencing in this moment is ok. Spiritual growth isn't about becoming something different. There is no significant progress for anyone who spends their time judging and rejecting aspects of themselves. Growth occurs when we stop dwelling within the restrictive positions of condemnation. Pure spiritual practice must involve a steady dedication to withdrawing identification from all positions, stories, thoughts, feelings and emotions that dance across the canvass of our consciousness. All are limitations if we become absorbed in them.

Believing we are insufficient blinds us to the fact that we are always given exactly what we need for growth within each instant of our lives. By turning awareness inward with the aid of this practice, growth is natural and spontaneous. We need only make the effort and allow Divine Providence to handle the details.

It is common for beginning meditators to be overwhelmed at how active and negative the mind can be. The temptation is to be overly critical of some of the things we experience - *"There are too many thoughts… How could I think that…? This isn't working… I'm getting nowhere… Maybe in some other lifetime…My programming is too strong…"* The ego loves to think it somehow got the raw end of the deal and that God somehow screwed up with us.

This common reaction can be easily overcome by sticking to the practice. This is why it is imperative to have a technique that helps draw awareness inward in the midst of any situation we happen to find ourselves. I always wondered why most meditation practices are strictly eyes closed practices. What do we do with the vast majority of the day where our eyes are open? It is much more effective to have a meditation practice that can be applied at all times, eyes closed and open in any situation, regardless of the condition of the mind or body. Meditation is most beneficial when it is continuous.

Do I need to give up my current religious affiliation or spiritual practice to learn?

No. The only thing required is the willingness to apply this practice as instructed. This is a teaching that conforms to your lifestyle and preferences rather than you needing to conform to it. If you are a Buddhist it will help you be a better Buddhist. If you are a Christian it will help you be a better Christian. Even if you have no spiritual or religious affiliation to speak of, it will still enhance your quality of life. Anyone can practice awareness regardless of what they choose to believe.

What if no thoughts come? What if there is no mind to notice?

'Notice the mind' does not mean there must necessarily be a mind, or thoughts, to notice. The intention to follow this step will naturally draw attention inward. This is the real purpose of Step One.

One helpful tip for your practice - rather than focusing on what your experience is *not*, instead accept the experience as it is.

How long should I repeat the technique?

As long as there is the tendency to become absorbed in the mind, it is of immense value. Imagine standing waist deep in a rapidly flowing river. Now imagine standing on the shore watching the river pass. By applying this practice, one becomes immersed in the stability of the Silence beyond change. At this point, thoughts pass by without affecting our peace. Many find that the Five Steps draw them immediately into a state of pure Peace regardless of the quantity or quality of thoughts.

During my practice how long should I wait before going back to the technique?

The moment you start thinking about it gently return to the technique. Awareness is more important than timing. As soon as you become aware that you can think the technique that is the ideal time to do it.

Could you explain Step 3? I am not sure I know what it means to 'Let It Go'.

This means to allow things to come and go as

opposed to clinging to anything. You may think the technique and let it go only to find it comes up again right away. This is perfectly fine. As per Step 4, 'allow whatever happens to happen'. Sometimes the technique will come up again immediately and sometimes it will fade away and other thoughts will arise. Sometimes you will end up coming back to the technique in rapid sequence and other times it will totally fade away. Either way, this is ok. The key here is to let go of control.

Can I use other techniques with the Five Steps?

There are some very powerful ones that can be used. The exercises in the workbook section of the book *A Course In Miracles* and the techniques of a practice known as 'The Ishayas' Ascension'[14] work beautifully with these steps.

If desired one can place their Star Word immediately after 'OM'. (i.e. OM *God*...OM *Love*... OM *Brahman*...OM *Buddha*...OM *Christ*...OM *Krishna*...OM *Peace*...)

It isn't suggested to verbalize or chant the techniques aloud. OM should not be drawn out, but just

---

[14] More information on The Ishayas' Ascension can be found in my book *Ascension Meditation – An Introduction and Guidebook.*

introduced simply and silently in the mind. Exactly as it is written we just think OM.[15]

Whatever technique is chosen, keep it simple!

Why 'OM'?

OM is an incredibly powerful and ancient Sanskrit meditation mantra. It is repeatedly referred to as 'the Supreme Mantra' throughout the sacred Vedic texts known as the Upanishads.[16] The teachings within the Upanishads have inspired spiritual students for thousands of years. They are Great Teachings of spiritual enlightenment.

Is it recommended to change the technique periodically or can I just stick with the Glory technique?

You can, but you do not have to. **Glory to ★ in the Highest** will always be powerful. Combined with your star word, it is one of the most powerful things anyone could hold in mind.

If you come to a point where you feel the practice

---

[15] It should sound like 'ohm' not 'aum'.

[16] There are any number of translations of the Upanishads available. I highly recommend – *The Upanishads – The Breath of the Eternal* by Swami Prabhavananda and Fredrich Manchester

isn't working then be aware - *it is only the limited agenda of the ego, looking for a certain experience, which has been disappointed by clinging to an expectation.* Some people bounce from one technique or practice to another trying to capture a certain feeling or mood that fits their preconceived notions. This is not allowing (Step 4 – 'Allow whatever happens to happen'.) but a noble attempt at 'my will' controlling.

Is there a preferred body position or posture recommended for eyes closed practice?

Above all, be comfortable. There is never any benefit in maintaining a painful posture. Especially if attention winds up focusing more on bodily discomfort as opposed to the practice itself.

In terms of alertness it can help to keep the spine straight, whether sitting or laying down. Roll over on your side and curl up in a ball and sleep may come quickly.

I find that I fall asleep no matter what posture I use with this practice.

When sleep comes, it is often entered at a much deeper level from meditation. Such deep rest can be quite healing at levels we may not be aware of. This practice will give us what we need. If that means we fall asleep then so be it. Perhaps it was exactly what was needed most at the time. We may have the intention to remain alert, but at the end of the day it is wise to allow what happens naturally without resistance.

I often get frustrated when I drift away on thought streams so easily.

Frustration only occurs when the agenda of 'my will' is not met. In the instant you remember to think the technique, it is helpful to not look back into the past at all – not even at what has happened a split second ago. There was a moment where you became *aware* that you *had* drifted. At that point, what you noticed has already passed.

Attentiveness to what is happening in this moment effectively takes frustration out of the picture as long as Step 4 (Allow whatever happens to happen.) is made the priority. The *allowing* of Step 4 cannot be done without the *awareness* of Step 1 (Notice the mind.). They go hand in hand.

I find that I am easily distracted by noise when I am trying to meditate with my eyes closed.

This is especially common for those new to meditation. Simply bring attention back to the technique when you remember. With persistence, this gets easier and you will find that you are less disturbed by external noises.

I once needed the quietest surroundings just to be able to read a book. Even then, my mind would wander so much I would have to re-read pages several times! My eyes would scan the words over several pages but I would be lost in thought. Now, it is easy to read with ease in the midst of a busy airport terminal and not drift away at all.

Noises become easier to deal with in meditation until you give them less and less attention. This is the key. Noise will always surround us to varying degrees. The real issue is - how does the mind react to the noise? The label of 'barking dog' may open the doorway to the commentary of – 'When will that stop? It's ruining my quiet time! I cannot concentrate with that annoying barking. That dog ruined my meditation...'

As the Stillness becomes clear via direct experience, it becomes evident that it cannot be disturbed by anything.

What more can you say about noticing?

Noticing means *to be aware*. Awareness can be defined as *attention without tension*. Noticing thoughts does not mean obsessive attention to their detail. Sometimes awareness of the mind can be like being aware of the dull sound of the passing traffic a few blocks away while relaxing on the sofa in the living room. You can be aware of the flow of traffic but the specific details of each vehicle are totally uninteresting.

In a similar fashion, we know there is mental activity occurring, but not much attention is given to it. Whether the thoughts continue or not – either way it is no longer important if we are allowing it to be.

What should I be looking for?

We don't need to worry about *what* we are looking for. What is important is that we are looking. That is, to be attentive. Ultimately, the act of being aware is its own reward. We aren't increasing awareness to acquire something greater. Awareness is our True Nature. So why seek for something else?

But shouldn't I be looking for peace?

The experience of Peace is the natural by-product of using the technique with the Five Steps. It is self-revealing. You don't need to search for it. Peace is synonymous with awareness. Awareness is silent and still. The awareness of stillness occurs in ever-greater depths as outlined in Section I. It is a depth that reveals itself quite automatically without the need to 'try to get deeper'.

Ultimately, the practice of present moment awareness takes precedence over the seeking of liberation. To chase after a future state of liberation is like trying to grasp a mirage. We only chase what the mind projects into a future moment.

Why does meditation seem so difficult at times?

This is mostly due to misunderstanding or resistance. Beginners often need to be patient and allow time to adjust to the practice. Many experience an internal voice of doubt that questions if you are doing it correctly. With clarity and consistent practice any sense of difficulty quickly becomes a thing of the past. Over time this doubt will disappear.

In the fullness of the silence there can no longer be any dullness, boredom, difficulty, struggle, conflict or tediousness at all whatsoever. Peace, joy, happiness and contentment are no longer dependent upon external conditions of any kind. Each moment is full and complete.

Resistances and control lead to a difficult and unrewarding practice. Any time you struggle with it, review the Five Steps and see which you are having difficulty with. Stick with it and keep it simple.

It seems rather hard to believe that one could live in peace and joy all the time.

This does not mean that you may not be sad if a loved one passes away. It does not mean that you will not be angry if your home was robbed while you were on vacation. It doesn't mean you will be excited about filing tax returns. Emotions come and go for us all. What we are concerned with here is the degree to which one lives continuously in a certain emotional energy field. Some people live primarily in the field of anger. Everything makes them mad and they seem to be bored if there isn't something to be angry about or someone to be angry with. Moments of happiness occur, but are short lived.

Others live in sadness or guilt most of the time. It is as if there is an addiction to that emotion. They have become a slave to it. Those living in a constant state of sadness will listen to melancholy songs and watch sad movies. All of which serve to perpetuate the dominance of that particular emotional energy field. Many who are stuck in guilt will not allow any joy to enter. It is as if happiness itself is a threat to a justified painful position – the belief that they are not worthy. What that justification is differs from one person to the next, but it is there nonetheless.

What this particular pathway addresses is how we can move out of those dominating fields of influence and into a higher level where joy and peace dominate. The field of joy and peace is immensely powerful. So much so that it is no longer possible to be chronically angry or sad. Depression and guilt cannot exist in this state either. One has risen beyond the gravitational field of their influence. Sure, there may be moments where a cloud covers the sun, so to speak. But that is a stark contrast to living in darkness with only an occasional glimpse at the radiance of joy.

How do I live in the now?

The only thing in the universe that is not 'in the now' is the mind. Awareness is automatically 'now' without any need for us to think about being present. By using this practice life 'in the now' is an automatic by-product. It is an inevitability.

But, I can't stop thinking my mind is driving me crazy.

Your mind isn't doing anything to you. *Your reaction to it is creating the perception of a problem.*

It is worth looking at how most of us view our mind.

For example, a painful sensation in the body doesn't *cause* a low emotional state, what our mind says about it does. *Therefore, the true cause of unhappiness is the deep tendency to believe in whatever the mind thinks, even if the thoughts create emotional pain and conflict.* This is another way of saying *attachment.* Anytime you are feeling down look and see why. Ask yourself – "What voices in my head am I listening to?"

To be aware is *to be conscious of.* By becoming conscious of the subtle, intimate workings of attachment to thought itself, we can begin to liberate ourselves from enslavement to it.

Let us take a closer look at how we respond to an experience. This may refer to *any* experience.

Suppose, for example, you find yourself faced with a rather strong emotion. Immediately following the awareness of the emotion, a **label** arises such as 'sad'. The label is then projected onto the experience. A split second later, **commentary** follows the label. Commentary is just another way of saying *story.* Oftentimes the story is nothing new – 'Oh no, I am sad again… I thought I was over this… Here we go again… Nobody loves me…I am lonely…Why do I feel this way all the time? I am sad because this happened and because someone did this to me…Meditation isn't working because I still have this stuff come up…'

Commentary follows the **label** in an endless feedback loop that further reinforces the perceived reality of the label. Within this dynamic, it becomes clear how a label is identified with and mistaken to be 'me' - 'I' am sad… 'I' am depressed'. This is how we become self-absorbed. Here we have identified the very roots of suffering and limitation.

By recognizing the label as it arises we can practice letting go of it. This is where this practice is such a priceless tool. Instead of giving labels undue attention, we instead place more focus on the technique. *Once the label is surrendered, the commentary falls silent.*

Whatever the experience may be while meditating, it isn't necessary to call it anything at all - 'Busy mind'… 'Boring'… 'Profound... 'Deep'… 'Shallow'… 'Flat'… 'Expansive'… These are all labels. The instant we cling to *any* label we reinforce the separate identity of the ego-self that believes it either *is* the experience or at least *has* it. Awareness does not require labels and commentary. It exists independent of them. Even the thought 'I am aware' isn't needed. Even the label 'experience' is unnecessary. We can be aware that we are aware without thinking 'I am aware'.

With the practice of awareness, it becomes clear how the past is projected onto the present. When we identify with a label, we open the door to commentary. Commentary is of the past. Therefore, the ego is a collection of past thoughts that are subsequently projected onto the present and into the future.

Labels and commentary also pertain to one's role in life. Many identify with their professions, possessions, experiences, addictions, illnesses, parental and social statuses. We will all maintain our roles, but we can just as well do so without wrapping up our identity entirely within it. *What we do in life is not what we are.*

Identification with a label can even become a self-fulfilling prophecy. If you are unable to sleep at night for a prolonged period of time you may begin to think, "I am an insomniac". Once you have labeled yourself thus, the commentary that reinforces the claim is never far behind helping recreate subsequent nights of unrest.

The cycle of labels and commentary all pertain to past moments. You may have slept poorly *before*, but tonight could be different. The likelihood is not so great if we continue to identify with the label 'insomniac' i.e. '*I am* an insomniac'. Built into that identification is the assumption that you will not be able to sleep well in the future. What we hold in mind has great power, for better or worse. And many result in a lack of openness to the possibility of a new experience.

By looking at this particular example from yet another perspective, we could identify a belief that a certain number of hours are required for optimal rest. If we don't get eight hours, we feel we are going to be exhausted the next day.

This meditation practice is perfect for sleepless nights. When you cannot sleep, meditating eyes closed with this technique will result in a great amount of rest and relaxation.

Are you suggesting that this technique is the magic pill that will solve all my problems?

A problem is only a story... a point of view... a position. For example, there is a difference between *alone* and *lonely*. Alone is simply a fact, whereas lonely involves an emotionally laced story of being sad and down. When identified with, the story creates the perception of a problem. One can be alone without an emotionalized story and all is well. We can be happy with *or* without others. Our innate happiness does not need to depend upon whether we have company or not.

To be aware of how we have been programmed and how to overcome it is the 'magic pill'. Meditation helps us prioritize higher awareness. Like an anchor in stormy waters, the technique has a tremendous grounding effect - especially when used each time by putting attention in the heart. As long as the awareness of Silence is not yet clear, the technique will serve to center us. It is what we come back to time and time again.

Besides the Five Steps are there other ways of doing this practice?

Just remember this – each time you think the technique, simply think it, let it go, and allow whatever happens to happen. If you stick to these basics you will be fine.

When you use the technique, there are two options of relating to the experience that unfolds – 1. My will be done (control). Or 2. Thy Will be done (allow).

My will fights with the experience and tries to force its agenda.

Thy Will allows and embraces what is.

My will never results in the experience of peace.

Thy Will only results in the experience of peace.

What are the benefits of regular meditation? How does life change?

This varies somewhat from one person to the next. Everyone will have his or her own unique experience of this practice. Some of the most common benefits are as follows:

- Improved sleep and rest.

- Decreased work and family related stress.

- Increased calm and relaxation begins to replace anxiety throughout the day.

- Enhanced spiritual practice and awareness

- Notable increase in inner peace, happiness, self-acceptance, stillness and contentment.

- An optimistic worldview begins to replace the 'cup half-empty' worldview.

- Greater empathy, compassion and love for others and ourselves.

- Many who are involved in 12-step recovery groups find meditation essential in helping overcome addiction.

I have tried to stop my mind, but nothing seems to work. Will this help me get rid of my thoughts?

This is arguably the most widespread misunderstanding with respect to meditation.

The attempt to rid the mind of thoughts seems to make perfect sense – "My thoughts are creating endless anxiety, so if I could only get rid of them I would finally experience peace". Trying to silence the mind typically results in wasted time and energy, with frustration being more the result than peace.

In the movie, 'A Beautiful Mind', the main character played by Russell Crowe lives much of his adulthood as a paranoid schizophrenic. During his life, there were certain familiar acquaintances that he maintained close contact with from childhood to adulthood. As real as they appeared to be, they only existed in his imagination. By the time he finally realized this, his promising life and career were nearly ruined.

His recovery is intriguing, because the imaginary acquaintances never actually disappeared. With the help of trained professionals, he was able to see them for what they were. While they may not have gone away, his *relationship* with them changed. As a result, they no longer had an adverse effect on his life. We all have a similar ability to shift our relationship with the voices in our own head.

With my meditation practice it seems like nothing is happening. I don't feel much peace or love. There is not much difference in the state of my mind. It thinks the same things that it always has.

Many spiritual students will go through periods of feeling this way. Transitioning from absorption in the ego-self to the Infinite Self is a rather significant shift. This involves letting go of the familiar and comfortable as we seemingly free-fall into the unknown.

Along the way there can be periods of profound changes that alternate with times where it feels like nothing at all is happening. It is not uncommon to experience periods where inspiration seems to have fallen flat interspersed with periods of passionate devotion. Through it all, regardless of what your experience is, it is important to remember what we wish for the most. Why did you begin this practice to begin with? If your goal is Self-Realization… to wake up… then there must be faith that whatever is happening is serving our growth and everything is in its proper place. Surrender to Divinity is the surest way to be free from the fetters of ignorance. Surrender means letting God write the script. Then all of life can be embraced with full confidence knowing that God Herself is orchestrating the dance of your evolution into more expansive states of being.

At times it may be easy to overlook how powerful this meditation is. Regardless of how you may feel, each moment that you apply the technique is highly significant. The difference can be so subtle that you may not notice anything at first. But it is within the subtlest shifts of perception that the most profound changes can take place. The shifting of even a single small stone can result in an avalanche.

At times it is tempting to look for changes that meet our preconceived expectations. From the surface of the mind it is difficult, if not impossible, to accurately gauge progress. Neither should we dwell too much on emotions. These fluctuate from one moment to the next. Feelings are a source of very *un*reliable feedback.

Your experience can appear unimpressive if you are looking for something that is not there. I have worked with people that can be aware of the Stillness, but they discount it in an instant and immediately look for something else because there are no fireworks, bells and whistles. They look past what is here and now, seeking something that fits their idea of what they feel should be.

Only the mind's commentary says, 'nothing is happening'. It is only a label that says the experience is 'the same' as another moment. It never pays to overlook Step 4 (Allow whatever happens to happen).

I thought proper meditation resulted in the experience of bliss, love, wisdom and joy. You have described it so, and this is what I have read and heard from other traditions and teachings.

That is absolutely true. These come from giving undivided attention to the experience *as it is*. If you aren't embracing what is, you are resisting it and harbouring a hidden position regarding what you think should be. As long as this position is held, there will be frustration. The only way to progress into perpetual joy is by surrendering all of your expectations and giving your attention to what *is* unconditionally. It is only by dropping our ideas of how the experience should be that we allow everything to unfold in its perfection.

How do I deal with intense emotions, thoughts, feelings and energy?

In moments of great intensity, do not forget this practice. Avoid using this practice to try and force an experience to change or be different. That is not to say the experience won't change at all. It may or it may not. This is not the point.

You may refer to the earlier explanation of labels and commentary. They are of tremendous help here. In a moment of intense anger, for example, the mind may run a thousand miles an hour. First, recognize that the reaction of anger is a program. Next, you may realize you are identified with it when you think or feel 'I am angry'. If you have become aware of these things, then perfect! You are already on Step 1 - *Notice the mind*. Just follow through with the rest of the steps. Notice the labels as they arise and where you attach to them via commentary. Recognizing this is pivotal to transcendence of their dominance. It may seem difficult or overwhelming at times, but, with commitment to the goal it gets easier to avoid getting swept up in the programmed reactions.

IMMERSION IN SILENCE

"Silence is the sole requisite for the realization of the Self as God."

Sri Ramana Maharshi

No matter how glorious and wonderful, a meditation technique is only a vehicle, a tool or a means to Self-awareness. Eventually one may find that tools of any kind are no longer necessary.[17] There comes a point where the experience of the Self becomes undeniably clear. One can be aware of it without the aid of any technique, mantra or practice. Even if it is not established in all moments, the Self is still clearly experienced whenever one remembers to be aware of it.

With this level of clarity, the way in which one practices meditation changes. In the past, the technique may have been relied upon as an aid to draw attention inward to Silence. Here the technique is no longer necessary as a means to access the Presence. The awareness of Internal Silence itself now

---

[17] 'When the fish is caught we pay no more attention to the trap.' Huang Po

becomes the practice and is experienced without any sort of process whatsoever. Communion with Divinity is direct and instantaneous and without any word or thought whatsoever.

While the pathway has simplified, the choice for Peace becomes even more important and paramount in all moments. The only mistake one can make at this point is to become lazy with practice and allow attention to become absorbed into thought once more. One must decide what is more important - thoughts or Silence? Ego-self or Infinite Self?

The first section of this book describes growing into the experience of the Self. The reason this was covered prior to outlining the practice is because there is no rule that any technique is necessary at all to become aware of Divine Presence. In fact, many have connected with it in their lives spontaneously, sometimes without even knowing it. Yet, it is so very rare for one to awaken to the Presence without a proven technique and never waver from it again.[18]

The following describes the nature of practice once the Stillness has become clear. The following instruction is outlined via 'Two Steps' for the sake of clarification. Unlike the Five Steps, these steps do not

---

[18] The great sage Ramana Maharshi is one rare example.

indicate a process, but a direct awareness. Those who share this experience will recognize that this is characterized by the purest simplicity.

THE TWO STEPS

1. Notice the presence of interior Silence.

2. Allow it to be as it is.

These two 'Steps' represent the very core and essence of devotion and liberation. This instruction only applies when there is a clear experience of Stillness and there is no longer doubt or uncertainty about the experience. In other words, *you know that you know it.* This is a knowingness that comes not from arrogance, but from certainty.

The ability to apply this teaching isn't indicative of an accomplishment, reward or achievement so much as a natural progression. It is a reflection of a refined state of awareness. Again, the Technique applied via the Five Steps may naturally lead one to this realization, but that doesn't mean the Five Steps are required first as a rule. Anyone with a clear experience of Peace may begin here.

Where absorption in the mind begins, the potential for direct awareness of Stillness ends. Where absorption in Stillness begins, absorption in the mind ends. It would perhaps be more accurate to term this section *Abidance As Stillness*. By consistently following these Steps the distinction between a 'me' and 'silence' dissolves until Silence remains as the primary identity.

The Two Steps have nothing to do with the mind, feelings, sensations or conditions. Even if the experience of Silence is not constant, that is ok. The only requirement is that the experience is clear when one remembers to be aware of it. Deeper and prolonged periods of silence come with continued practice.

1. NOTICE the presence of interior Silence.

Simply be aware of the silence. This is all.

Avoid focusing on what it looks like or feels like. Silence is formless. It is not an object or a feeling. Commentary creates an illusory sense of separation between a commentator and the experience. To whom does the experience occur?

2. ALLOW it to be as it is.

Only the ego-self is unwilling to allow. It puts up resistance in favor of its own preferences.

One accurate definition of the ego is – **E**dging **G**od **O**ut.

Avoid focus on what the experience is *not* – "Not deep enough…Not as expansive as before…Different than yesterday…" Much commentary is focus on what is perceived to be lacking. In addition, *all commentary arises from the appearance of separation.*

By pro-actively engaging these steps in all moments we allow Divine Providence handles the details of our spiritual evolution. We step out of the way, and in doing so we discover joy.

QUESTION AND ANSWER

Is there any value in using a specific technique or object for meditation at this point?

The greater the awareness of silence, the greater the power of what is held in mind. The power of any mantra, thought, prayer, meditation or contemplation practice is enhanced when held in mind at this point. So there may be value to using some of these even though they are no longer needed as an aid to draw attention to the Stillness.

In the midst of a chaotic situation one may choose to focus attention on harmony, love or compassion and, in doing so, contribute in a positive and powerful way to the overall field of consciousness in which all are intimately connected. This is done not to control or manipulate a situation, but to uplift it for the good of the whole. What we hold in mind has the power to manifest in our lives – whether it be positive or negative. Therefore, one must be cautious and choose wisely.

No matter how 'advanced' one may be, it is forever wise to remain attentively engaged in. At any point there can be the potential to fall back into old, limiting patterns. This is also where there can be value in using a technique. It can help us stay on the straight and narrow path. With regards to our spiritual evolution there is no finish line. Growth continues forever. Along the way it is easy to grow stagnant and plateau within a certain comfort zone. The best practice is to follow the Two Steps vigilantly. If the heart's desire is to continue to grow, then the necessary arrangements will be made by the Higher Self for that to occur.

I find that sometimes I cannot get as deep in my practice as I would like.

'Getting deep' has nothing to do with you. If you are preoccupied with having a deeper experience than the one you are faced with, place more attention on *what is* rather than *what I want*.

Trying to get deeper is a sure way to remain stuck. Great moments of expansion occur when force and effort are surrendered. Such moments are always a gift of Grace and never a result of personal force.

If internal Silence is my true Self then what is it that notices it?

Only the Self can be aware of the Self. Internal Stillness is indicative of Divine Presence. There is not anything other than That which is even capable of awareness. It only *appears* as if something other than the Self is aware.

It is like the analogy of peering deep down into the darkness of a deep well. Sometimes it feels like we are experiencing Silence 'deep within' from 'up here' on the surface of the mind. It is as if we are bouncing around on the choppy surface of the sea of thought where it appears as though Peace is somewhere deeper, as though 'I am here and Silence is down there'. The only thing creating this perception of a separate 'me', which appears to be limited in time and place, and which appears to be separate from the fathomless depth of internal silence, is attachment to the mind's commentary and labels.

Pay attention to what the mind is telling you and what you are believing. Absorption in commentary will isolate the experience of separate 'me' into a limited point of reference located in time and place. It is amazing how it can appear as though there are three different distinct parts of ourselves – thought, silence and 'me'. It feels as though this 'me' bounces around between the thoughts and stillness, as if in limbo. It is all an appearance. Like a dream, it only seems to be real when we are caught in it.

So, I am the witness of thoughts?

With regular practice of the Technique with the Five Steps, the quality of witnessing develops naturally. It is an important and significant step to be witness to thoughts and feelings instead of being absorbed in them.

Eventually, the identification with being the observer must be relinquished. By clinging to the identity of being the witness, the appearance of separation arises between the witness and that which is witnessed. While an important step, at some point it becomes clear that this is a limitation. As practice evolves into regular application of the Two Steps, any identification of being the witness falls away. When absorbed in silence, it becomes clear that the whole notion of 'witness' is nothing more than a concept.

How will I know when I can move to using the Two Steps instead of the Five Steps?

When the experience of the Self is clear and can be experienced at any moment without the aid of a technique, and you are *certain* that what is experienced is indeed the Self.

On one hand this is a natural progression, on the other hand clear guidance often will prove to be critical. I have seen many people who have meditated for many years and feel stuck. Some even had access to a very clear experience of Peace but chose instead to search for something to match their preconceived ideas. The mind is so very slick that it will always look for what it wants to see; seeking whatever matches its expectations. Clear guidance will help identify the perils and rewards of effective practice.

The Way of the Mystic is a pathway of *un*-doing. This involves discarding all the ideas that only lead us to chase mirages of our own making. Be content let go of every thought stream that seeks to define you or God. Let go of the incessant commentary that would attempt to define your day or current situation. Constantly empty yourself of all these things and bring attention back to the Five Steps as instructed. On the straight and narrow spiritual pathway there are not 10,000 things you need to do. This practice is simple and only gets simpler as we let go. All complication is of the mind. What is needed will come as long as one is intensely vehement.

'Be Still and lay aside all your thoughts of what you are and what God is, all concepts you have learned about the world, all images you hold about yourself.

Empty your mind of everything you think is true or

false, or good or bad, of every thought it judges
worthy and of all the ideas of which it is ashamed.

Hold onto nothing. Do not bring with you one
thought the past has taught, nor one belief you ever
learned before from anything.

Forget this world, forget this course, and come with
wholly empty hands unto your God."[19]

Sometimes it seems this practice is difficult for me.

It is not the practice itself that is difficult so much as
the resistances of the ego that make it appear difficult.
If difficulty arises, it is likely you are having difficulty
with one of the Steps. The most common difficulties
involve misunderstanding or resistance.

Once the basics of this practice are understood, all
that is needed is to return to them time and time
again. This alone will carry one forward. Even if your
thoughts are telling you how hard it is you can still
apply the steps anyway.

---

[19] From *A Course In Miracles* - Lesson 189

If the Peace of God is the reality of all things isn't it dualistic to say 'interior silence'?

No matter what the experience may be, always bring attention inward. This may sound paradoxical, but it is from that internal experience that we let go of labels such as 'Internal Silence' or 'External Silence'. There is a habit of calling the experience a *this* or a *that*. This is where the separation of duality is formed. The purest experience of the Silence is always discovered within.

Are the Steps the same thing as surrender?

All Steps and instruction have been presented in the name of surrender to the Higher Power/God by whatever name one would choose to call it.

While Practicing the Two Steps it is best to avoid...

- ❖ Allowing the ego to claim credit for accomplishing something. Silence is not an object that is acquired. Peace has nothing to do with the ego.
- ❖ Perceiving Silence as a gain or reward. To whom is it a gain or reward?

❖ Taking it personally if the experience of Silence isn't as deep and full as it was in a past moment. Comparisons with the past blind us to the freshness and aliveness of the present moment.

❖ Trying to recreate a particular experience from the past, or trying to force the current experience to be a certain way.

❖ Attachment to any and all preconceived notions of 'liberation' or 'enlightenment'.

❖ Subtle commentary that places you somewhere in the Silence – 'I am in the Stillness…I rest in the Silence'. This is like looking out into space and projecting a fixed point somewhere where no such point exists in reality.

❖ All conceptualizing about God and spirituality. Fancy descriptions on a menu do not satisfy hunger… A sign pointing in the direction of Paris is only a sign pointing in a direction…When the Stillness is clear, it is a total waste of time to dwell upon thoughts and words.

❖ Seeking a particular feeling or sensation to go along with the experience of Peace. The incomprehensible vastness of outer space is not dependant in any way upon a shooting star. The fleeting may be enjoyed but don't let it draw attention out of that which is permanent.

The Two Steps and Self-Enquiry

Self-Enquiry is the spiritual practice taught by the great sage Ramana Maharshi.[20] This involves looking within to discover the source of 'I' and meditating on that as a means to liberation or, Self-Realization. The 'I' that Maharshi refers to is not the thought of 'I' but the awareness of one's beingness. Each thought arises out of the field of silence. So, Self-Enquiry is another way of saying - *awareness of silent being-ness beyond thought.*

It would be incorrect to practice Self-Enquiry by focusing only on thoughts of 'I', 'I am' or 'I exist'. Instead, we allow these notions to pass while maintaining attention on the silence out of which they arise. The thought that says 'I exist' is not required in order to be aware of one's own existence any more than we need to continue thinking 'I am in Central Park' over and over again while taking a walk in Central Park. It is a silent certainty.

Self-Enquiry is a means to abide in the pristine state of the birth-less and death-less Self. It is only when identified with thought forms that the true 'I'

---

[20] For a fantastic reference to the life and teachings of Ramana Maharshi see *Be As You Are – The Teachings of Sri Ramana Maharshi* by David Godman

subsequently becomes an 'I am this' or 'I am that'. At that point, we lose awareness of silence and become entangled in something other than that.

Without a clear experience of Silence, Self-Enquiry can be difficult. This is commonly the case when we are in the midst of activity. It is not that the practice itself is difficult. It is supremely simple! But the attraction to thinking tends to be so very strong that attention wanders easily. To break this wandering habit, two things are needed – certainty and vigilance.

First of all, it is imperative to know that you are practicing correctly. When doubt prevails there will be no Peace. It is only when one is certain that they can be truly vigilant in the practice. The practice of Self-Enquiry and the two 'Steps' described in this book are the exact same thing. If you wish, you may simply call them both 'Awareness of Silence'. This is the essence of this teaching.

My own practice of meditation began with the practice of Self-Enquiry. But when I first attempted it, I constantly questioned whether I was doing it properly. It seemed like a struggle in the early stages as my mind was so utterly restless. Fortunately, Ramana Maharshi also advised those who struggled with Self-Enquiry to learn to meditate with a technique until one becomes confident enough to transition to Self-Enquiry.

HEALING APPLICATION

The mind is often the most turbulent during periods of physical discomfort. Sickness, injury, chronic pain and terminal illnesses can all dredge up a whirlwind of conflicting thought streams; piling emotional distress on top of painful sensations. This is where this practice can serve as a powerful tool. Many wonder - *Can this practice result in physical healing?* It will increase the likelihood, but it doesn't guarantee it.

Emotional healing, however, *can* be effectively cultured anytime. The key is to be aware of the causes internal distress. Emotional stress is created by absorption in mental commentary. What are your thoughts telling you about the situation? What is your relationship with those thoughts? To shift relationship with any pain or physical discomfort involves changing our relationship with commentary.

This practice will help make this transition easier. To that end the technique, **Glory to ★ in the Highest** and the Five Steps will be used the exact same way as previously described. But instead of placing attention in the heart each time we think the technique, put attention directly onto the physical discomfort itself.

This should be done as simply as possible. It should not be any more difficult than thinking of your big toe, for example. If attention wavers from this practice, gently bring attention back again. There must be no strain or force involved.

You will notice the dialogue about the pain may be rather intense at times. Let it come and let it go. Don't fight with it and don't try to avoid it. Be aware of labels, 'headache', 'backache', 'arthritis', 'old joints', 'the cold that is going around', 'toothache', 'allergy', etc. If you let the label go, chances are commentary will not be as intense. But even if both the label and commentary arise constantly like a persistent gadfly, one can still refrain from fixating on them. If you don't label the painful sensation what is left is just pain. And we can even let go of the label 'pain'. Then, what follows is awareness that is simply aware of a sensation. Awareness minus attachment to commentary is silent and still.

If one can be aware of the Silence - to the degree where the Two Steps can be applied with confidence - one can remain attentive to pain while remaining simultaneously aware of the Silence. The essence of devotion and liberation is to remain attentive to Silence no matter what happens. In reality, there is not one single thing in this universe that has the power to draw us away from the Silence.

I do as you advise but the pain only increases…what do I do?

Allow whatever happens naturally to happen. We cannot force the experience to be a certain way. We may wish to be pain-free, only to find there is pain in spite of our best wishes. If we cannot control the experience the only thing left in our power is to let it be. Of course, it is always wise to seek whatever treatments are available to us – holistic, medical, homeopathic or otherwise. This instruction is not intended to be applied in place of any means that would aid in accelerating physical healing. The point of this instruction is that one can abide in a state of peace and happiness no matter what is happening in the mind or the body.

Many of us have become quite adept at *avoiding* the present moment. There is the habit of checking out and resisting certain things. Resistance only draws one away from the path to freedom. We must learn to embrace all that comes in each moment. This does not mean to be complacent! There is nothing as pro-active and engaging as the practice of awareness.

With greater attention in the present, there are times

where thoughts, emotions and pain will appear to intensify. Living awake can be jolting to anyone who is accustomed to being asleep. The truth is nearly all of our thought streams were attempts to avoid this moment.

I find that I get headaches on occasion when I do the practice.

The one thing you can do if headaches are common is to at least make sure you aren't forcing the practice. Best rule of thumb - keep it simple. If the headache persists don't waver from the above instruction.

It is hard to focus when there is too much pain.

Only remain aware of the movements of the mind. If you think 'It is hard to focus' when such and such happens and you believe that thought, it will become a self-fulfilling prophecy. Start over fresh in each and every instant. With meditation the simpler we make it the better. There is no moment where awareness cannot be aware – that is simply not possible. Awareness is supreme simplicity and is just another name for meditation.

There is no moment where one is not given exactly what they need. There is no moment where we are lacking. Everything is in its right place. Sometimes we reach a barrier when we think 'I can't'. But that is a decision, a choice. Why not choose differently? Is the barrier out in the world, or is it in you?

PART III

By simply being open to seeing things differently, we can more greatly appreciate the multiple facets of the diamond otherwise known as the human experience. The explanation given in this Section is not an attempt to give the right answer. It only offers some perspectives and ways of looking at ourselves, our experiences, our spiritual path of choice, and our life differently. Perhaps the best way of articulating this is with an example -

A few years ago I decided to try mountain biking for the first time. For several months, I mostly rode the same kinds of trails on the same kind of bike over and over again and never seemed to tire of this. Then, one day I watched a video of some very experienced mountain bikers, which expanded my understanding of what was possible. Soon afterward, I rode with others who had many more years of experience than I did. When I finally returned to my trails of choice I was amazed to find my experience of that same mountainous terrain, which I had ridden so many times, was now totally different. It was as though mountain biking had become brand new to me all over again. By simply being around others with more experience resulted in an altogether more rewarding experience than before. (If we disregard the epic wipe-outs!) This was all due to being open to another perspective.

It is easy to get caught in a routine in our lives where, without knowing why or how, we become closed to seeing life differently. It is more common for us to see things the same way over and over again. In place of innocence, the mind takes over and tells us how everything must be from moment to moment and from one day to the next. Just a tiny bit of humility is all that is required to open the door to a new way of viewing everything. Nothing drastic needs to change to return to innocence. After all we are already imbedded in the wonder and glory of Creation. The willingness to see things differently is all that is necessary. When one is open to receive, the means will be presented.

Do not read the following with the purpose of merely disagreeing, agreeing or adopting my perspective blindly. No part of this should stand apart from personal experience. Being open to seeing things differently does not mean you will see them exactly as I do.

Purification and Transcendence

Purification means to replace negativity with positivity. Any practices, techniques or teachings that help strengthen positive thinking are of immense value. They help to enhance our self-esteem, optimism and overall satisfaction. In place of pessimism, gratitude and appreciation begin to prevail. The power of gratitude is utterly transformational. And is such a simple choice. If we are grateful, we aren't complaining, when we are complaining, we aren't grateful. The former is a position of great power and the latter is one of weakness.

As upward-spiralling attitudes prevail, there may be occasional relapses into negative patterns. While this is common, such tendencies become less frequent. The power of positivity is very attractive. Its rewards are immediate as well as long term. Life becomes much more fluid, productive and fulfilling. It becomes clear that we are not victims to the circumstances of life. There is a growing appreciation in realizing that the thoughts we choose to listen to have great power. We can now recognize the wisdom in the saying - "Be careful what you wish for" - as one does indeed attract what is held in mind. The fact that this becomes acknowledged is indicative of a significant leap in consciousness.

As consciousness continues to evolve, at some point a conflict arises. The very statement or belief that "I create my own reality" is called into question. Not because it isn't true, but it is more the question of exactly *who* or *what* is it that is creating or manifesting? What exactly is the 'me' that has channelled its 'personal will power' to manifest the life that 'I' want?

While the power of the mind has been acknowledged, one may still believe that fulfilment is dependant upon certain external conditions. We may still believe we can be happy only if the universe re-arranges itself to fit our pre-conceived notions of how we think things should be. This is not bad or wrong in a moralistic sense. But it is a limitation. Any happiness or love that is thought to depend solely upon conditions and circumstances will remain impermanent. The joy of the Infinite Self is utterly without conditions of any kind. It is our programming that projects conditions outward onto the world where none exist in reality.

The 'I' that has assumed that it was in control often remains intact throughout all the positive changes in self-esteem. With spiritual maturity comes decreased reward derived from trying to force the universe to match our limited notions of happiness. What emerges next is an increasing desire to know the real 'I', which is the source of True Power.

The source of True Power is impersonal, unchanging and is the source of the ego's presumed personal power. Alignment with anything other than 'Thy will be done' will never lead to any lasting measure of joy or fulfilment. Therefore, liberation consists of handing over personal will and everything that was ever thought to be 'me' over to God.

With 'my will' in play, life can evolve toward a great degree of mental purity and effectiveness, but never permanent peace, love and joy. With mental purification, there is still identification with the mind/body/personality, the confines of which have only become more pleasant.

The state where negativity dominates can be likened to living in a dark grey prison cell with no furnishings and only a simple mattress upon which to sleep. Mental purification is like having new carpet installed, the walls painted, a soft bed, comfortable chair and a large flat screen TV with a fancy cable package. While the difference is obviously great, this doesn't change the fact that it is still a prison cell.

Consistent attention in the Silence is the only way to experience freedom from mental imprisonment. Transcending the mind is altogether different than the purification of the contents of the mind, which, at best, only help to make life in limitation and separation more pleasant.

Again, this is by no means an attempt to downplay the value of relative purification. Each step away from negativity is powerful. But it is important to recognize the limit of personal effort along the spiritual pathway.   As long as the ego-mind's agendas dominate, the likelihood of future suffering exists. At the same time, the perceived separation from God will remain intact. The realization of the presence of God within as the infinite Silence is true purification. True purity isn't gained or added, but is what remains when the identification with the ego is surrendered.

Ignorance and Enlightenment

Ignorance is another way of describing the state of being unaware of Divine Presence. Enlightenment is the state of being aware *as* Divine Presence.

Terms such as 'enlightenment' or 'liberation' are only appealing when we are not currently experiencing the Presence. In the Silence, these labels are of no interest. But, 'from the outside looking in', so to speak, there may be great interest in elaborate descriptions of enlightenment and that which stands in the way of it.

The Self-aware mystic is not interested in any labels at all, much less any idea of being enlightened. When the wellspring of Silence is full and complete there is no felt need to call it a *this* or a *that*. It would only be the ego-mind that would add commentary to the experience. Only the ego-self would declare itself enlightened. That which would declare such a thing has been removed from the picture with true enlightenment.

Sin

Sin refers to the choices we make in life that create distance from God. There is only one 'sin' and that is mistaking illusion for reality. All of us have fallen short of the glory of God by mistaking illusions for reality at some time or another. Contrary to popular belief, God neither punishes nor rewards anyone for his or her actions. Our actions are followed by *consequences* for which we are accountable. The consequence of pouring water in your gas tank is a vehicle that will not run. The malfunctioning vehicle isn't punishment, but the result of an ill-advised decision. The result of a healthy diet and exercise is a healthier body. Good health is a consequence of a particular set of choices and actions.

The consequence of mistaking illusion for reality is the potential for suffering in some way, shape or form. For an infinite being to confine itself within the limitations of the mind, the consequences will always be less than fulfilling. God doesn't care if you remember Her or not any more than the sun cares if you wave at it every morning or not. Whether you choose to acknowledge its Presence or not, is up to you. An omnipotent, omniscient and omnipresent

God gains or loses nothing either way. But what we stand to lose cannot be described in words. It's tragic, to say the least.

Sin cannot be mentioned without also mentioning ignorance. It is in the innocence of not knowing better that we are often *unaware* of whether the choices we make are taking us further from, or closer to Divinity. That is why the Way of the Mystic necessarily involves the vital element of *awareness*. We become conscious of our choices and strive to choose wisely.

Like the prodigal son, we can all turn back toward the Light at any time. The love and fullness that await in the glory of Divine Presence are not rewards… but your very essence.

The Soul vs. The Self

Common definitions of the soul include beliefs in separation from God. Therefore, it would be incorrect to assume that the soul is the same thing as the Self. Of course we have a soul, just like we have a body, but it is not the sum total of what we are. Even though the soul exists prior to, and will continue on after the passing of the physical body, it is still subject to change and alteration. By contrast the Self is beyond all name, form, change and alteration.

The highest purpose of our soul's existence is to acknowledge the presence of Divinity in all moments and in all things. If you ever wonder 'Where is God?' the answer is 'Everywhere'. To acknowledge this is like a wave acknowledging the vastness of the ocean, realizing it is not possible to ever be apart from it in reality. Like 'wave' and 'ocean', 'soul' and 'Self' are only mind-created labels. Many of our ideas regarding the 'soul' are maintained by ideas we have read about or heard from others in the past. The Divine Self has no need for nametags and historical references.

The soul can be likened to an invisible energetic body that attracts to itself experiences and opportunities for the sake of conscious evolution. Via moment-by-moment choices within our various experiences, the soul evolves, remains stagnant or devolves.

Through all the choices and experiences throughout the course of its evolution, the soul becomes imprinted with propensities that determine the overall context for any given lifetime or moment. It is not so much the experiences themselves as much as it is how one reacts to them that determine a soul's progress, or lack thereof. Therefore choice is everything. This is why the wise have always encouraged and instructed students along the path of Truth to 'choose wisely'. There are consequences to all actions and decisions. None of the ripples and waves from individual choices is isolated in their effect. All have an impact upon the whole of creation.

Love and Acceptance

It would be unrealistic to think we can experience love on a regular basis without overcoming the tendency to believe we aren't worthy of it. Often there are 'justified' reasons why we feel unworthy. But are these justifications based upon reality or fantasy? There is not one single program that deprives one of the experience of love that is of any value at all. Any such program only serves to uphold the limitations of the ego-self. They do <u>not</u> reflect the true nature of the Divine.

You may notice that there are some aspects about you that you accept and some that you condemn, some parts that you believe are lovable and those that you feel aren't. This is how we can identify programs where self-worth is lacking.

The thought processes that view parts of us as unworthy of love are often self-*hating* programs. We have become brainwashed into thinking we couldn't ever possibly be worthy of the love and acceptance we long for. Maybe in some things we feel we are worthy, and yet other parts of ourselves, no, certainly not! This perspective is backed up by stories and commentary, which rationalize our viewpoints. We may thank past experiences and the conditioning of society for helping create such insanity.

The pursuit of love can be viewed the same way we commonly view the search for peace and happiness. That is to say, love is typically sought 100% externally. To fill the emptiness inside, love and acceptance are sought within family relations, intimate personal relationships, sexual encounters and casual interpersonal friendships.

Because we believe love is dependant upon external conditions, we assume it is bought and sold via 'right' behavior. Therefore, we become frantic seekers of approval. We learn to modify our behavior to elicit the hoped for response from others whose affection we crave. We begin to feel good about ourselves only if others feel good about us. We allow ourselves to be affected by praise or blame.

This perspective of love is emotional dependency. Conditional love is dependant upon particular circumstances that we project onto the world. We become dependant upon the ego's perception of appropriate conditions. All those parts of ourselves that we deem unlovable and unworthy are pushed aside, supressed and hidden.

Un-conditional love is a concept that is talked about far

more that it is experienced. Un-conditional means: without conditions. *Love without Conditions = Reality.* Imagine the rising sun shining in all her glory, but we didn't see it because the curtains were closed. The sun doesn't care if we live in darkness or not. Either way, she does not withhold her light. It is us who have put restrictions in place. Whether or not we open the curtains depends on us, not the sun. The sun has no investment in the matter.

The way to live in the clarity and reality of unconditional love is via *acceptance*. Ego-self's perception of love is 'Only if…'. The Reality of Love without conditions is 'No matter what.'

Love is not an acquisition but a certainty that prevails when all conditions are removed. We do not need to figure out how to love unconditionally. We only need to let go of all those belief systems that have kept the imaginary restrictions in place. The technique given in this book, used via the Five Steps results in a state of acceptance (Notice…allow…). By consistently putting it into practice, the result is condition-free peace and love. Opening the curtains doesn't *cause* the sunlight to appear, it reveals it. Removing the imaginary conditions doesn't cause love. It doesn't result in us obtaining God's approval. It allows the ever-present love of God a means of entry.

As Father Anthony deMello so brilliantly put it, "Nothing surpasses the holiness of those who have learned perfect acceptance of everything that is. In the game of cards called life one plays the hand one is dealt to the best of one's ability. Those who insist on playing, not the hand they were given, but the one they insist they should have been dealt – these are life's failures. We are not asked if we will play. That is not an option. Play we must. The option is how." [21]

---

[21] *'Taking Flight – A Book of Story Meditations'* Anthony deMello, S.J.

The situation in which you currently find yourself is the ideal one for you in terms of opportunity for optimal growth. Therefore, karma is a gift. Perhaps more practical words to use in place of karma would be 'accountability' or 'consequences'. It is naïve to assume that anyone could ever act without consequences.

Most feel as though they are victims to circumstance. Victim mentality in this world seems to be the rule rather than the exception. The belief in victimhood is so deeply ingrained that it is rarely questioned. At some point we have all felt that life has blown us around like a leaf in the wind. Deep down, victims essentially believe the world is unjust, God-deprived and imperfect. It is a hopelessly bleak outlook without substance or merit.

Victimhood, while essentially limiting, is also predictable, safe and comfortable to the programming of the ego. As long as anyone believes they are victim, they can always blame someone or something else for any undesirable results in life.

The payoffs that are derived from victimhood appear

to be endless – lawsuits, sympathetic attention, justifications for laziness, unemployment, etc. All these 'rewards' are poor substitutes for the true power of personal accountability.

Ultimately, all are responsible for their own level of happiness. Victim consciousness is rooted in illusion. We are influenced by what we choose to hold in mind. Karma is what was meant by the Biblical verse, *'for whatever a man sows, that shall he also reap'.*[22]

It may be tempting to look back into the past and wonder why or how you could have attracted certain situations into your life. It is common to hear people bring up endless examples of the suffering and cruelty of the human race such as – 'If there is a God, then why does 'He' allow these things to happen?' The truth is, we can never know the bigger picture or purpose of a certain event. Judgment always guarantees a limited perspective. Great good can arise from tragic events.

There was once a pessimistic young woman who made regular visits to her doctor for help with her depressed emotional state. The best the doctor could do was write a prescription to treat the depression. As it turned out, this did little to change the woman's

---

[22] Galatians 6:7 Lamsa Bible.

cynical view toward the world. One day, during a routine breast exam, the doctor discovered several malignant tumors and a double mastectomy was required to remove them. A couple of months later, one would never believe her incredible transformation. When faced with her own mortality, she realized how precious life was. Her amazing transformation into a bright, joyful person was inspirational. Without the experience and challenge of having cancer that change in attitude might not have taken place.

Another way of looking at the nature of karma is to know that it is not different from the mind. Step beyond the mind and you step beyond karma. Each time you engage the mind, you step back into the cycle of karmic change. It is said that the discovery of our true infinite Self is like roasting all the seeds of karma. Once a seed is roasted it will no longer sprout. Karma is like the cosmic learning curve that has been steering us toward awakening all along...

Exalted Experience

Exalted experiences arise as a result of the refinement of the senses of perception. Some are born with a heightened sensitivity to the subtleties of creation while others may develop this through spiritual work. Some characteristics of exalted experience involve enhanced intuition, the ability to sense others thoughts and feelings, celestial perception, sensitivity to energetic phenomena, past life recollection, healing abilities, psychic abilities, out of body experience and the ability to see auras.

Exalted experiences are also characterized by sensitivity to beauty. The taste of food becomes more exquisite, the colors and vibrancy of physical surroundings is heightened, the sense of smell is refined to the point where the fresh bloom of spring is richer than ever, an orchestra or opera is more deeply appreciated. What once appeared to be ordinary is now alive and vibrant. By living ever more fully in the present moment, all of life is experienced in greater clarity. The richness of feeling gradually replaces dry intellectualizing. Overall, it is an awakening of all the senses. Many mistake this for the state of enlightenment itself.

The potential trap of exalted awareness is to be caught in the external, and non-physical, forms of beauty and wonder. It is possible to experience much of the above without having the foggiest notion as to what the true Self is. Many have spent lifetimes dabbling in exalted experiences and are just as identified with the ego-self as those who have never had any exalted ability. In fact, many supposed spiritual paths have as their primary objective the goal of attaining special abilities such as miracle powers or telepathy.

Because these experiences can be so impressive and even otherworldly, many make the mistake of thinking that they have awakened, become enlightened or have arrived ("This is it!"). The key point to remember throughout any experience or newfound perception is – The purest experience of Divinity is found within. It is silent, still and unchanging and may not have all the bells and whistles of the exalted realm. It is possible to discover it and hardly have any exalted experiences to speak of. Life can even continue to appear quite normal. Some are more sensitive to exalted experience than others. It is best not to worry about it. The surface experience of life will be what it will be. Whether or not you can see auras or remember a past life is unimportant.

Worship and Meditation

As long as worship involves a subject/object relationship with God, it will only reinforce the illusion of separation. Often worship involves the belief that one can win the favor of God and avoid punishment via appeasement and genuflection. To assume that that which is omnipotent, omniscient and omnipresent needs flattery or even cares if it is remembered or not is an absurd notion. This is like offering up a lit match to the sun. The Almighty lacks nothing.

Many scriptures warn against worshiping idols. *Any* image of the Divine is an idol. This is so whether that image exists in our minds or sits and collects dust on the mantle above the fireplace. The advice not to worship an idol was never meant to be an order, but a very helpful suggestion. Many worship idols without even knowing it. This is what happens when one clings to a system of beliefs about God instead of pursuing direct experience. The words and thoughts themselves have become the idol of worship.

This certainly does not mean sacred images are without value. One can admire the image of a great Saint and be inspired to follow in their footsteps and to live their teachings. Reading a powerful teaching from a great scripture like the Upanishads, Dhammapada, Bhagavad-Gita or the New Testament can uplift and inspire one to take the High Road in life. Sitting in a chapel or ashram can be a transformational experience. Admiration and devotion tend to go hand in hand.

To the true mystic, any worship that involves a subject/object relationship with God is of no interest. It has been replaced by dedication to the *essence* of what all sacred images point to. Admiration only grows for the Great Teachings and Teachers who have inspired the masses by their lives and examples. The purest spiritual teachers, mystics and masters never sought to be worshipped at all. Their teachings were put forth so that the student could *live* the essence of the teaching. The true teacher only helps the student remove any imagined distance between themselves and God.

While meditation may very well include sacred images, its aim is not to flatter the image or put them on a pedestal. One may use an object for practice in the beginning, but as the Two Steps point out, the image is usually transcended as consciousness evolves beyond the need for it.

Where does traditional prayer fit into this instruction?

No prayer is without value and effect. What prayer means and the form it takes tends to change as consciousness evolves. I used to think that prayer was only about apologizing for my actions, asking for the things I wanted in my life or rote recitation of the Lord's Prayer. There was fear that God would punish me if I forgot to go through the motions.

A more powerful and worthwhile form of prayer involves focus on gratitude and appreciation rather than on what appears to be wrong or lacking. This doesn't mean that you don't pray for the well-being of others or the betterment of the world. It does not mean that personal desires or wishes are suppressed. It is never of any use to pretend that they don't exist. By bringing the focus toward appreciation and gratitude, the perfection inherent in all things becomes apparent. This form of prayer is its very own reward in that we begin to see that every part of our life is already the most precious gift.

Renunciation and Desire

Many spiritual and religious teachings speak of overcoming desire. Such instruction may give rise to the notion of abiding in an idealistic state of desirelessness. Pretending desire does not exist or that we are not influenced by it when we really are is blatant denial. We cannot be free and at peace by fooling ourselves. If we demonize desire and make it wrong, we only remain caught in yet another limiting position.

It is far and away more effective to *understand* desire. To do this effectively, we must be willing to take an honest look at ourselves. This involves being willing to look at what we feel would bring about a state of fulfilment. It can be discovered that there are ways of viewing desire that are conducive to growth. After all, desire and growth are not incompatible.

For most people, the search for happiness is directed outwardly, into the world of form and change. Seeking fulfilment externally is only natural if there isn't the experience or knowledge that the greatest source of contentment can be discovered within us. Spurred on by our conditioning, we look with longing upon the things that we feel will fill an inner lack.

Desire is a projection of our values outward onto a person, place, thing or situation. We are happy if we get what we want, and disappointed if we don't.

Often, the object of our desire may be exciting and fulfilling at first, but soon loses its appeal. Then it's off to the next thing. One easy place to see this is in how some people approach relationships. Many are addicted to the high of the honeymoon phase, but have trouble committing beyond that. Desire is then projected onto the next potential partner or, more accurately, onto the ideas we have in mind about how the ideal partner should be. Like this, we chase our happiness from one perceived ideal scenario to the next.

To attach fulfilment to something outside ourselves means we will only be content if situations arrange themselves to fit our ideas. It is not possible to overcome this by supressing desires. Rather, one must be aware of the dynamics of what is happening within the mind. This is best done by becoming aware of the conditions that our programming imposes. Externally seeking happiness involves the belief we can be happy *only if* such and such happens. Our projected conditions are limitations that allow the Divine little entry into our lives.

Renunciation is often advised as being an integral aspect of any pathway to the Divine. Historically, this notion has been plagued with misconceptions, often leading some to abandon personal belongings, jobs and family. True renunciation isn't of possessions, but of control. The great sage Huang Po said it beautifully, "*The ignorant eschew phenomena but not thought; the wise eschew thought but not phenomena.*"[23] As with desire, the key is understanding true renunciation. To do this we look at its opposite, *possessiveness*.

Possessiveness, or ownership, is a state of mind. It is possible to be surrounded by possessions and inwardly remain non-attached. By contrast, it is possible to give up every material possession and still remain just as attached to the positions of the ego-self as before. Real possessiveness doesn't refer to physical objects, but to where we cling to programmed positions. Real renunciation consists of is surrendering the attachment to those positions. As Huang Po pointed out, this is an inside job.

When we cling to *only if's* we cling to *my will be done*. This is where the core of control can be identified. When life is no longer restricted in this way one can flow along the river of Grace instead of resisting the

---

[23] The Zen Teaching of Huang Po by John Blofeld

currents.

How to Co-Exist Sanely With Desire

1. Acknowledge the desire whatever it may be. Do not resist it.
2. Be open to it not happening or manifesting. God may have a better plan.
3. You do not need to know the details of that plan. It may be bigger than can be comprehended.
4. Choose to accept that desire will manifest if it is for the highest good of the universe and not just for you.
5. Realize that we are blind and asleep as long as we remain attached to a particular outcome. We can be just as blinded by aversions, as we are attachments. After all an aversion is simply an attachment to 'what I *don't* want'.
6. Be very open to not getting your way. As far as I can see, this is the best medicine for sanity.

Out of Body Experiences (OBEs)

The out of body experience (OBE) is a very real phenomenon. While an OBE can happen anytime, there are certain conditions, which increase the likelihood of their occurrence. Many books[24] have been written on this topic so we will not explore specific techniques regarding how to create this experience here. But it is important to know a bit about OBE's due to the fact that many have had them occur spontaneously while practicing meditation. It is not an uncommon phenomenon. Given my own experiences as well as those of countless people I have worked with over the years, I felt it necessary to add some perspectives on this topic.

When I first experienced some of the phenomena associated with OBEs, I didn't understand what was happening. There were periods where I would wake up momentarily paralyzed, yet fully alert. Intense and odd buzzing/vibrating sensations would arise spontaneously. Energy would flow up my spine and head. Sometimes it would be a subtle sensation and other times like a loud reverberation. Powerful

---

[24] Such as books written by William Buhlman and Robert Bruce

rocking sensations were so strong there were moments where I thought an earthquake had started. Occasionally, while laying on my back meditating, I would realize I had rolled to my side only to find out that my physical body was still laying flat on its back. There is nothing quite like hearing your nose breathe out where you thought your ear was! There were times when I would get up from meditation only to find the body was still laying on the sofa.

After a few years I became aware of testimonials from others who experienced some of the exact same phenomena I did. This helped put some things in perspective. The strange vibrations and energetic sensations often accompanied leaving the body as if the etheric body was vibrating itself out of the physical body. At times I would not experience any peculiar sensations at all as I lifted ever so gently and effortlessly up from the body like a feather floating in the breeze.

Many make leaving the body a goal. Support groups exist in order to assist others in creating these experiences. To this day I do not know why I had those experiences. I never went into eyes-closed meditation with the intention to exit the body. Initially I wondered if I was imagining or dreaming these things. But after dozens of OBEs, I could no longer doubt what was happening.

After working with hundreds of people from all over the world I began to see that meditation isn't the only way conditions for an OBE can arise. The following represent certain situations where they b are very common.

Trauma Induced OBEs

Reports of OBE's are common in hospitals where patients have reported floating above the table while their body is being operated on. Subjects report being very alert and aware in this state and are able to listen in on the conversations between the surgeons and can describe the operating room in detail.

Some find themselves suddenly out of body in the midst of a harrowing accident such as an automobile crash or near drowning. Countless trauma induced OBEs could be listed here ranging from drug overdoses to cardiac arrest and it seems there are testimonials from people who have suddenly found themselves out of the body right when the physical situation became the most intense or stressful.

I met several people over the years that developed a tendency to live their life slightly outside their physical body. Some reported leaving their body during past moments of physical abuse where they witnessed the phenomena while floating above. Prolonged exposure to intense stress can lead to a state of more regular detachment where one lives for long periods outside of the physical body.

In such cases, the OBE has become a way to escape intense emotional and physical pain. Subsequently, with repeated exposure to abuse or stress, this became a way of living - a means of avoiding the deep emotional scars. Effective spiritual practice can heal one's relationship with past emotional scars. One can then re-enter the body and begin to experience life unencumbered by the past. This healing does require forgiveness and the overcoming of fears. At the end of the day, it is absolutely worth it.

Intentional OBEs

Many are intrigued with the idea of being able to leave the body at will. It is fascinating and liberating to float about without a physical body. The more one exits the body, the easier it becomes. With practice one can become quite adept at it.

While this may all sound fascinating we only have a physical body for a little while. So, it would be wise to embrace the physical world for the short time we are here. It is possible to be adept at leaving the body and grow very little spiritually speaking. And it is possible to evolve by leaps and bounds and never leave the body at all.

The most significant opportunity for spiritual growth occurs *within* the physical body – in how we approach each moment, in how we treat others, how we come to understand ourselves, and how we share ourselves with others.

The Astral

OBEs can open the doorway to non-physical realms where dis-embodied entities congregate. Some leave the body in order to explore these realms and visit with spirits or seek information from supposed 'Ascended Masters'.

It is important to be aware that just because an entity is not in the flesh does not automatically mean they are perfectly pure in their intentions. Some do not have your best interest in mind. Discarnate beings are not saintly by virtue of the fact that they are discarnate beings. The naïve assume that just because a being doesn't have a body, they will somehow have all the answers for us here on earth. There seem to be no shortage of channelers of astral entities who dabble in these realms. In our innocence, we have no way of knowing what we are really dealing with in this world, much less the non-physical realms.

Curiosity draws many to astral travel. Initially, there is fascination with the fact that there is more than just the physical universe. For many people there is the desire to contact a loved one who has passed. Then there are those who resist life on earth for whatever reason. The momentary periods of escape are felt to be liberating. *True* liberation cannot be found through resisting or running away from anything, therefore this form of liberation is only a temporary form of excitement and entertainment. Whenever we run from our problems, we are bound to them.

Some believe that spiritual advancement looks like having the ability to leave the body at will and visit astral realms. For some, this can even become a prideful badge of achievement. Many erroneously equate this ability with the supreme state of enlightenment itself.

The true mystics have always advised against dabbling in these realms. This is especially important if one desires to discover the presence of the Divine. If this is your desire, the only thing you need to remember about the astral realms is - *Don't go there.*

OBEs as a means of escape and avoidance

Motivation for leaving the body often arises due to resistance or avoidance. Some people simply resist being in a physical body. Negativity, difficult life situations, physical and emotional pain and a burdensome, uncooperative body are all very common reasons for wishing to escape. However, that which we run from follows us like a shadow. Leaving the body does not mean that our suffering is automatically transcended. Why? Because if we run from a thing it is due to a position we hold internally. That position remains until it is understood from a higher level of consciousness. As the saying goes, 'What you resist persists'.

If one constantly resists life, there is no openness to seeing God in all things. Sure, pain and resistance can be great at times, even overwhelming, but there is nothing that devotion to Divinity cannot overcome. With faith it really is possible to move mountains. Among the most powerful practices of the mystics is the decision to be content and happy no matter what.

'Just Being in the Now' vs. Being in the Now with a clear experience of Silence

It is quite possible to 'be present in the now' with no awareness of the Self and believe spiritual enlightenment has been reached. Of course 'being in the now' is a vital part of this practice. However, one can be attentive to the present moment and not have a clear and confident experience of Divine Presence. Everyone goes through this phase. But the hardest cases are those who are convinced they know it when they don't. Some even mistake an aloof state of detachment for liberation. The fact of the matter is, *anytime you feel the goal has been reached; you are caught by another ego position.*

It is vital to be clear that what is experienced is actually the Infinite Self. The mind is so very slick it can even doubt that. At this point, guidance is very important. One must be <u>clear</u> about the experience - not to get a pat on the back, or to feel as though we have arrived, but to remove doubt about it. Then one can direct all attention into the Silence with confidence. One must become as clear and confident about the experience of the Self as is the diver who has no doubt when he has plunged into the ocean.

There can be no true liberation without this degree of certainty.

The Zen Teaching of No-Mind

In the Stillness of the Self, there is neither the mind nor any form whatsoever. It is easy to read some of the popular Zen teachings that refer to 'no mind' and assume that one must work to try to still the mind. This assumption can lead to much wasted time and energy on trying to calm the waves of thought rather than letting them be and instead, choosing to dive beneath them.

The Self is utterly still. Thoughts do not disrupt it. Our attraction to thoughts draws attention away from it. Those with sufficiently advanced awareness will be able to discern between the mind and the Silence with ease. As the Silence is made the priority in each moment, the mind may eventually stop of its own accord but not because there was any effort involved. Whether it continues or not is unimportant. Silence is not dependent upon conditions – not even the condition of the mind being active or not.

The great source of confusion with the notion of 'no mind' is the belief that one must first silence the mind in order to become aware of the Self. All too often, this leads to a lot of effort and trying – all based on the hidden belief that "because there are still thoughts then I must not be making progress" or "I must not be doing this right."

The best attitude with respect to the mind is *active indifference*. This means to be fully attentive, but without investment in how we feel it should or shouldn't be. We can be as indifferent to the mind and its thoughts as the dance floor is with respect to the dancers.

Traps of the Spiritualized Ego

One shocking thing that I noticed when I attended my first meditation retreat was how questionable behavior could be so easily rationalized to innocent and naïve students via spiritual rhetoric. This was my first insight into how the ego can become spiritualized. To say it another way, ego-self can continue to operate just as it always has, but it does so with enlightened concepts. The core of it is there all along - the ego-self seeks to be right, feel important and be in control at all costs. To overcome it takes great honesty and humility. Some of those who present themselves as authorities may be just as lost as the students they attempt to guide.

The ego is slick enough to twist any new spiritual concept or understanding into a whole new identity and belief system. This is very common in spiritual groups and circles where some students, in spite of having the best of intentions, wind up replacing their non-spiritual conditioning with spiritual conditioning. This means the words and ideas are there, but the experience is minimal, or altogether absent.

In some circles, the jargon seems to catch on like wildfire. We are so accustomed to filtering everything through the mind that we do so with spiritual teachings as well. Perhaps a big part of it comes from the belief that spiritual advancement means we will become something different. There is also a deep driving need of the ego to be recognized or feel important. This is sought through the attention and approval of others.

Many consider themselves 'advanced' who have only attached to a new ego identity such as - being the person in the know, being a spiritual guide or teacher for others, the one who has been there and done that, one who has meditated for x number of years, someone who has attended a teacher training, advanced retreat, studied with this or that guru/master, etc.

At the same time, one who isn't caught in spiritual ego can be a direct, confident, clear authentic student and/or guide. The following will help one become aware of some common spiritual ego positions and characteristics so that they can be avoided.

'Why Am I Creating This?'

As we grow in understanding, accountability becomes more important than positions of victimhood. And yet, there may continue be things that cause one to feel as though they are a victims. One may be at a loss in trying to understand how they could continue to find themselves in the same undesirable circumstances over and over again. It is easy to feel like a victim to the ego-mind itself. You may wonder… 'Why am I creating this'?

If it isn't clear why a certain situation appears over and over again, it does no good to try and figure out 'why?' A much better approach is to pray for understanding. Trust that all will be clear if and when it is meant to be clear. The Higher Self is actually orchestrating this dance of evolution, not you. If you really need to understand why a thing occurs, never doubt that it will be made evident when the time is right and not a moment before.

To try to figure out why you are creating a situation is to engage in conceptual thinking which is the one place liberation is never found. Just assume that all that is happening is only so you can wake up. This is the one and only answer we need. When details need to be known, they will be known. When they don't, then all the forcing in the world will only push clarity further away.

'There is no right or wrong/good or bad.'

The belief that there is no right or wrong is a potentially dangerous position. One can potentially justify any behavior with this concept. This notion tends to ignore the fact that there are consequences for which one is accountable. If one is particularly self-serving, this rationale can draw inauspicious consequences to both themselves and others.

Sometimes those who engage in this sort of thinking have withdrawn from the perceived limitations of religious dogma only to swing in the opposite extreme – one where an 'anything goes' attitude prevails. This is a recipe for disaster in that it will not liberate one from the ego, but instead will only make it bulletproof. Be aware where this perspective is used to justify the ego's positions! The mystic has no desire or need to wander around thinking or saying 'there is no right or wrong or good or bad'. In the utter completeness of the Self there is nothing to justify.

The premise for this statement is legitimate - If God is omniscient, omnipresent and omnipotent, then there is nothing God is not. Therefore all actions are God's actions. But the million-dollar question is - Is one operating from an *idea* or the actual *experience* of this?

100% of the time the danger of this particular trap comes from operating under an idea of Divinity.

Benign Superiority

Just because you find something that works does not mean that it will be everyone else's path as well. It is arrogant to view people as being less than for not adhering to the same spiritual principles. Best to leave your ideas of what others should be doing up to God. To walk your path and dance your dance without feeling holier than thou is all that is necessary. Many are inspired to share their particular faith, spiritual practice and discoveries with others. This can be done without feeling morally superior and without being attached to others seeing things the same way as you.

The mystic may freely offer teachings like water from a well, but they do not attempt to coerce anyone to drink from it. They do not feel smugly superior if someone walks away uninterested. While their dedication may be to make their teachings available with great love, it is entirely up to the student to accept them or not.

Identity with Labels and Experiences

Relinquishing identification with labels is a necessary

practice if liberation is the goal. Any time we have identified with a label, there will be a sense of separation. Once we become attached to a label, the door to the mind's commentary is opened. The commentary then re-enforces identity with the label. It is a cycle that reinforces an ego-based sense of self.

In our meditation practice, we may label the experience in a multitude of ways – *still, busy, full, empty, same, different, changing, deep, shallow, etc.* Then there are the labels the spiritualized ego creates such as – *Shaman, Spiritual Teacher, Fledgling Meditator, Advanced Meditator, Recovering Catholic, Mystic, Light Worker, Co-Creator with God, a reincarnation a great being, Master.*

We all play various roles in life and our spiritual path is no different. One may go from seeker to finder to teacher. Nothing may change that fact. But one can play a role in life without holding onto a concept of becoming something special. The only thing that wants to become something is the ego. The path of liberation involves stripping away all presumed identities and emptying oneself of everything. In the Silence there is nothing to cling to, nothing to hold onto. One cannot cling to mind-created identities and dissolve into the Silence at the same time. This is why the path of liberation is often referred to as 'the straight and narrow path' [25]

The desire to become something different

Many adhere to an idea that they will eventually become something different with spiritual practice. Initially is not necessarily a negative thing. After all, this desire tends to drive one to make necessary changes in their life, which facilitate growth. At some point this desire is seen to be a limitation. Ultimately nobody becomes something in particular when the Infinite Self is discovered - the wave doesn't change when it recognizes it is one with the ocean. What shifts is identity, not appearance.

Many long to be somewhere along the pathway other than where they are. This can lead to fervent seeking and striving for an ideal state where it is believed that all will be well. Whether your mind tells you that you are either 'not there', or 'getting there', this means that you aren't 'there' now. Furthermore, the 'there' that we are seeking becomes the proverbial carrot on the stick – forever beyond reach. The mind, which is itself a maze of limitations, is the only thing that

---

[25] "Enter in through the narrow door, for wide is the door and broad is the road which leads to destruction, and many are those who travel on it. O how narrow is the door and how difficult is the road which leads to life, and few are those who are found on it." Matthew 7: 13-14 *Lamsa Bible*

projects fulfilment into the future. So the 'carrot' is a limited ideal.

The tendency to project an idealistic state of being into the future all comes from a belief that there is something lacking in *this* moment. If the very notion of lack is mind-created, then refuse to go along with thoughts that tell you there is something lacking or wrong. By believing them, we project our happiness into some other moment.

The important thing is to use what tools and practices you have to the best of your ability in this moment. Divine providence will handle all the details so long as we remain steady and vigilant with our practice. It is wise to assume that a perfect God has created the perfect set of circumstances for growth.

Detachment from the world – How aversions can become more noble than attachments.

I went through a lengthy period of being very detached from the world. During this time, I either ignored or avoided 'worldly' responsibilities, believing they were distractions. I believed I had more important things to do than deal with credit card debts, family, working 'ordinary jobs' and filing income taxes. At the same time I looked at all the material things I thought I was attached to and promptly got rid of them. Soon I was down to a couple suitcases.

Scarcity was seen as an advantage because if I ever wanted to suddenly up and go I wouldn't have anything tying me down. The intention was noble – to allow the Universe to provide what was needed. But I wasn't open to allowing the <u>full</u> abundance of the universe into my life while I maintained any patterns of avoidance. Of course, I did not see them as avoidance. I thought I was 'surrendered' and just 'letting go'. For some time I remained unaware of the limitations of the very positions I believed were liberating me. Aversions are every bit as restricting as attachments. At their core, both aversions and attachments are the egos positions of control.

Things that were seen as too material or worldly were simply not dealt with. To deal with them was viewed as a compromise to my spiritual path. I was afraid to commit to a job, a lease agreement on an apartment or a vehicle payment as that would tie me down for a certain period of time. And did I ever have an aversion to being tied down! My relationship with my wife was strained at times as well, due to neglect. The path I followed in order to become self-*less* became a very self-*absorbed* thing. I failed to see that true

Liberation is not dependant upon external conditions. Even as I had read about Buddha's recommendation on the 'middle path' so many times, I did not become aware of what that meant for some time.

Eventually I chose to embrace all those things I had neglected. Instead of ducking away from debt, I just saw that it was a sign that my life was imbalanced. Debt was not apart from God, but the very voice of God yelling at me to 'wake up'! As such, it was a gift.

By choosing to face all the former aversions with joy, a whole new and incredible dimension of life opened up. Aversions only exist when we are unwilling to see the Divine in certain parts of life. I chose to embrace the debts, the taxes, and a 40-hour a week job, as well as family relationships and all that comes with 'ordinary' life. Without realizing it, I had drawn a line between what I perceived to be spiritual life and what I viewed as ordinary life. Upon realizing this I began at once to erase any differences. As a result abundance in all areas flowed with little effort in ways I never imagined.

I once heard a story that someone saw an image of Mother Mary in a subway bathroom. A long line of people formed so that they could see the appearance upon the tiles. A reporter asked a priest what his views of this were. He responded by saying there was no way that Mother Mary would appear in a subway bathroom.

It is we who decide how and in what form the Divine will appear in our lives. But this decision does nothing to Reality. To believe the world is flat or the sun is cold does not make it so; it merely distorts our view of what is.

Intellectualized non-duality

The core instruction of all non-dualistic teachings, a.k.a. *advaita vedanta*, points out that the entire universe is only the Infinite Self. Not an Infinite Self *and* an ego-self. Not illusion *and* Reality. Not a changing universe *and* unchanging silence. Not even ignorance *and* enlightenment. All these differences are only dualistic perceptions. There is only the one Supreme Ocean of Divinity in which multiplicity is but an appearance.

While this is true in the absolute sense, **very** few underline experience this directly. A teaching that states 'There is no teacher, no teaching and no student' really doesn't really help the average person deeply entangled in conflicting programming. Furthermore, that statement only begins to make sense for those clear enough to practice the Two Steps outlined in this book.

Even so, there are many who parrot the teachings of great Teachers. Some even present themselves as Teachers themselves. Yet, for many of them, their words only actually reflect a conceptual understanding rather than the actual experience of the presence of Divinity. The pure Teaching and Teacher is the Silence. Without the direct experience of this, words don't come close to conveying the essence of the pure Teaching. The Presence *behind* the words is everything. A sports car without an engine is just a fancy shell.

The essence of the teaching of non-duality is the High Teaching. There are indeed pure teachers who are articulate and embody the Presence. And yet the false parades as the genuine article all too often. It is easy to become adept with the terminology of non-dualistic teaching enough to 'win' any argument and sound convincing. It is even possible to believe one has reached a high state of consciousness when no such thing has actually happened. Be careful! To try and win an argument, or put on a clever show, all comes at the expense of discovering a Fullness that will render such childish endeavour to the highest ranks of the absurd. Even an ounce of humility will end the charade.

To avoid the trap of intellectualizing non-dualistic teachings, the key is brutal self-honesty. What is your experience *really*? Is there any attachment to being right? To being understood? To winning arguments? Or in being perceived by others in a certain way? Do you still experience conflict and emptiness? Do thoughts still have the power to disrupt your peace? Do you experience the Peace that prevails in spite of anything that happens around?

Intellectual non-dualists can get caught by 'just being in the now' without experiencing identity with internal Silence. Those who experience the essence of non-duality have no care in the world at being understood, winning an argument or sounding clever. As the experience is full, there is no feeling that anything is lacking.

'Since all is the will of God, my will is already God's Will'

Without exception every person I have heard repeat this has done so from a concept rather than the experience of what this really means. How to know if it is one's experience? Pure surrender to Divine Will results in wordless absorption in Silence. Many who repeat this phrase are only doing so to justify some sort of ego position. This sentence really doesn't mean anything until one is absorbed in the experience of Silence. And in the experience of Silence this notion doesn't mean anything.

The Bulletproof Monk

This refers to one who has a heavily guarded self-image. Using clever enlightened concepts, the bulletproof monk can explain away any questionable behavior and convince others, and themselves, that their actions are OK and that there is a higher reason for the things they do. The most notorious cases of this exist with those in a position of spiritual authority. Some spiritual students who may consider themselves advanced may fall into this behavior as well, especially if there is investment in wanting respect and recognition from their peers.

Personally, I have seen some of the most bizarre behavior justified by individuals in positions of spiritual authority and large groups affected time and time again. Sometimes it seems the naïve are drawn to the irrational like moths to a flame. Whether non-integrous action is justified as 'taking on the karma of students', 'teaching the student a lesson' or 'helping them let go of enlightenment looking a certain way', there are countless ways that control masquerades as authentic guidance via clever rationalization. Things really get out of control when students begin to justify their spiritual guide's questionable behavior for them.

There is no shortage of accounts with regards to how power has been misused by authority figures. Many books are written on this very topic.[26] In every case, the motivation has been for gain of some sort. This gain can be to satisfy urges for power, sex, money or status. Or it can be gain in the form of approval, emotional dependencies or in attachment to being perceived a certain way, such as the object of others admiration. This leads to a heavy investment in projecting an image of infallibility rather than the honesty of 'what you see is what you get'.

Any ridicule from others is turned back at them as being 'just ego'. This is the very fabric of the bulletproof facade as the teacher/authority figure can act however they please and anyone who disagrees 'doesn't understand' because, after all, they aren't experiencing the same enlightened state the teacher allegedly is.

Spiritual students can have their own bullet proofing

---

[26] Such as *The Guru Papers – Masks of Authoritarian Power* by Diana Alstad and Joel Kramer

to protect themselves. Much of it we have discussed already. Other symptoms include – defensiveness, lack of honesty, projecting an image of what enlightenment and purity is thought to look like, not handling criticism well and turning away any honest feedback. Additional motivation for maintaining a façade is to attempt to mask deep emotional pain. This is a way of protecting oneself.

Basically all bulletproof monks are the same in that there is a rather strong attachment in being perceived by others in a certain way. The façade can exist to mask insecurities and to set oneself apart from others. With the bullet-proof guru, the teaching might be of unity and oneness but there still exists the felt need to set themself apart by finding ways to make oneself more special, in order to justify a position of authority.

Students can let their spiritual ego set them apart from others who aren't of the same tradition, religion, teaching or mind-set. Anyone who sees things differently are dismissed – 'they don't understand'.

To overcome this aspect of the spiritual-ego, humility and self-honesty is essential. This takes tremendous strength and courage. One can win over the approval of others and lose their soul in the process. The 'gain' of what others think is a weak substitute that comes at the expense of the source of true Freedom.

Seeking for gain

A spiritualized ego seeks to control outcomes just like a non-spiritualized ego. This inclination comes from the belief that fulfilment can be gained outside of oneself. By looking over the above examples it becomes clear with most traps of the spiritual ego, external gain is the motivation.

Through the practice of self-awareness, certain patterns can be identified. When recognized, one must avoid the additional trap of being harsh and judgmental toward oneself. All these traps are only programs. To recognize a program is empowering and helps to identify - what is the hoped for gain?

The spiritual ego may not be overtly negative at times, but it is still strong enough to keep one caught in false ideas. Awareness and honesty will continue to open doors. There is nothing pure devotion to Truth cannot overcome.

Comparison with others

Most spiritual students have experienced this to some degree. Maybe there is a peer in a study group that seems to be really getting it and you wonder why you are left in the dark. Perhaps you compare your path to an admired guru, saint, sage, spiritual teacher or leader. There is no shortage of books claiming to be true accounts of individuals on a grand spiritual adventure that seem to have amazing experiences and awakenings every time they close their eyes to meditate.

The best advice here is to focus on your path. Comparisons with others come from limited understanding and perspective and, as such, they are potential traps. Everyone has his or her own unique path. Comparing ourselves with others means we deny both the perfection of who we are and our very unique path in life. The sincere in heart will not be left behind.

QUESTION AND ANSWER

How can I be free of fear?

Many of life's most worthwhile moments come when we are willing to step out of our comfort zone and take a risk. Maybe it was the first time you asked someone on a date; or the first time you took a trip to a new and unfamiliar place. Maybe you made a decision that was not popular with family and friends but it was what was most important to you. In every case we must move beyond a barrier of fear to move toward what is desired.

Giving in to fear can lead to a life that may be predictable and relatively comfortable, but at the end of the day, not wholly rewarding. Yet many are content with this. Most people do not readily welcome change. An alteration in the status quo tends to bring about a knee-jerk response of anxiety or panic. Instantly, the ego-self works frantically to put things back into familiar order so that it can maintain a sense of control. This ensures the continuance of the mundane and repetitive while stalling the potential for growth. Life in the comfort zone may feel safe, but it is not liberating. One has closed themselves off to all that appears to be threatening, even if it is the very thing that is desired above all else.

The comfort zone is characterized by the fear of loss and the fear of gain. The fear of loss may involve money, family, friends, approval, life, etc. But there is also fear of actually getting what we want. One could say they desire something, but deep down there is a fear of getting it because that very thing may be perceived to threaten the status quo of our comfort zone. You may desire to unconditionally love and yet the truth is that many are secretly terrified of this. So many have a difficult time simply saying, "I love you" even to close family members. Not only that, but unconditional love first requires self-love and acceptance. This is something that isn't always easy for most people. One could desire a relationship more than anything but when the opportunity presents itself it might be shied away from simply because of the comfort and predictability of being alone. To be alone might not be fulfilling but at least you don't have to risk the possibility of being rejected.

The fear-based borders of the comfort zone are the boundaries of the ego's control. I have met so many people that tell me, "I just want to be free of fear." The implication is that, "If I am free of fear, then I can do what I want", or "…then I can commit to my spiritual practice more deeply", or "…then I can be truly free". Why wait for fear to disappear before acting? If everyone waited for fear to be gone before doing anything great nothing great would ever be accomplished. By facing fear and choosing to walk through it, the doorway to expansion opens up in unforeseen ways. It is a sad fact that people die every day not having had the courage to go for their dreams or follow their greatest desire in this life.

Anyone who walks through fear will find that it was much smaller than it initially appeared. In fact, by walking through it, it may even dissolve completely. I was once so terrified of public speaking that I was a disaster while giving presentations at school. When I began speaking to large groups as an adult the same fear would continue to arise, but I chose to ignore it and continued on in spite of it. If I had waited for the fear to go before speaking, I would still be waiting while life passed by. Most of the things I feared initially never came to pass and if they did, I figured that I would rather fail giving it my all than to not try at all.

So many allow fear to win and settle for less. To the ego-self, fear is very real. To the Self there is no such thing. Given there is only one Reality and that is the Self, *fear can never be real.* To live under the shadow of fear is to surrender to a phantom. Commitment to

Silence will lead to the dissolution of the fear-based comfort zone of the small self.

I try to let go of judgment but it comes up constantly anyway.

Let the mind do whatever it wants, you don't have to listen to it. Even with all the judgmental thoughts you can still be totally free of judgment at the same time. Just don't make judgmental thoughts special. If you allow them to flow through without clinging to them they will have no effect. Remember Step #4 - Allow whatever happens to happen. Be aware of the label – 'judgmental thought'. Following this label, the commentary says 'That's not a good thing. I must be going nowhere with my practice…'". Drop the label and there will be no problem.

All judgment comes from a limited perspective. By passing judgment, there is the assumption that, "I know the bigger picture and all the factors that play into this single event." Only God knows the bigger picture. The mind is incapable.

How can I develop true love and compassion for others and myself?

Through self-acceptance. The technique taught in this book along with the Five Steps will help anyone culture self-acceptance automatically if put into consistent practice as instructed. The very nature of *allowing whatever happens to happen* with the practice opens the door to love and compassion - first toward ourselves, then this flows outward effortlessly to others.

True compassion involves the necessary ingredient of unconditional love. Unconditional love is revealed by removing conditions. The only place in this universe where conditions exist are in the mind. The peace, joy and love of Divinity have no cause or conditions of any kind. Like the radiance of the sun, they simply *are*.

Many of us have the stubborn tendency to constantly reject parts of ourselves consciously or unconsciously. There is a tenacious belief that something is wrong or out of place - that who or what I am is not good enough. This can even become a self-*hating* tendency and is therefore a form of self-violence. There is no fertile ground for love or compassion to blossom as long as consciousness remains polluted with such self-abusive indulgences.

Maybe the notion of accepting all parts of yourself seems difficult at first. If your desire is to be free of restrictive conditioning, the most effective way is to allow *all* thoughts, feelings, judgments and commentary to be as they are without labelling or resisting them. Unconditional acceptance is the highest form of self-love.

Isn't the idea of self-love a bit egotistical?

This depends on which self you refer to. Infinite Self lacks nothing. It does not seek love from an external source in order to fill an internal void. Ego-self perceives lack and seeks to fill the void by attempting to acquire love externally. Those who do not experience a depravity of love in themselves can very well *share* love with immense joy. But those who feel a deep lack seek to receive it from others.

Far from being egotistical, true Self-love emerges in direct proportion to the decline of the ego's dominance. When love is lacking, ego-dominance is obstructing it. To be self-loving means to distance yourself from programming that restricts and distorts the reality of love. Ego's version of love puts limitations in place by saying it can be possible only if such and such happens. It views love and happiness as acquisitions, which must be bought and sold through behavior modification.

Most people believe that love and happiness are dependant upon conditions of approval from others. At the same time there is the persistent fear of rejection. So we constantly run from one phantom and chase another. Fearing disapproval, we chase approval. We attempt to present ourselves in a way that we hope is accepted by others. All the while, fear of failing and not being worthy hides in the shadows and serves as the puppet master for our behavior.

How do I know if what I am hearing is the voice of God or the ego?

The purest experience of the voice of God is *Silence*. During meditation, it would be unwise to make a habit of listening to any internal voices at all. The voice of deception can wear a very clever and convincing mask. The desire to discern God's voice clearly comes from a desire to be led in the right directions in life.

Trust that if there is something that the Universe is trying to tell you, then that message will be made clear to you in some way, shape or form. If it is important to you, then an all-powerful God has more means at her disposal than hushed whispers. Avoid limiting the voice of God to some special isolated experience. Divinity is omnipotent, omniscient and omnipresent. Therefore, the voice of God is everywhere.

The more I meditate, the more I have expected my emotions to be less intense but this is not my experience. When will I be free from painful emotions?

Let go of the labels - 'depression', 'sadness', 'anger', 'intense' etc. Without a label, whatever moves through awareness is no longer 'this' or 'that'. When nothing is labelled, one experience is no longer more or less special than another. It is what it is. Try this for yourself and you may just find that *no label = no story and no story = no problem.*

All labels are stories from the past. A thought may arise about 'how miserable I am' and suddenly, '*I'm* sad and depressed and have been for x amount of minutes, hours, years...' 'When will I stop feeling this way?' 'I'm sad because of ...'. In the blink of an eye, a label opens the door for a story, which in turn justifies the existence of the label.

The practice of meditation weakens identification emotion. If there is an emotion we can see where we identify with it when we think '*I* am angry' or '*I* am sad'. If the 'I' gets caught and absorbed in this feeling, we think we *become* our experience. The way out is through awareness. The instant you catch yourself identifying with *any* thought or feeling, simply return to the meditation technique and the steps. This will help pull you out of it.

What is the experience of the Self like?

It is uncaused fullness, silence, aliveness, joy, love and bliss. It is without form at all whatsoever. The reason the term 'Self' has been used generously is because this uncaused Presence is experienced internally as being the very core and essence of our being. At the same time, it is entirely impersonal, existing beyond all dualistic notions, such as 'me' and 'it', 'self' and 'Self'. Self is immune to time, birth, death and age. It is forever untouched by the ebb and flow of life. [27]

There is no flatness to be found within the fullness of Divinity. The beauty and perfection of each moment

---

[27] "Thou shouldest know that real sanctification consists in this that the spirit remain as unmovable and unaffected by all impact of love or hate, joy or sorrow, honour or shame, as a huge mountain is unstirred by a gentle breeze." *Meister Eckhart*

are experienced to such an extent that it actually becomes quite difficult, if not pointless, to cling to any thoughts of the past or future. What is discovered is a really sweet, fortuitous and mysterious flow to life. The great spiritual teacher Anthony de Mello S.J. stated:

"All mystics – Catholic, Christian, non-Christian, no matter what their theology, no matter what their religion – are unanimous on one thing: that all is well, all is well. Though everything is a mess, all is well. Strange paradox to be sure." [28]

Words cannot come close to describing what the presence is like any more than a menu can give a taste of the food. It would be tragic for someone to starve to death while holding the menu. This is what happens when concepts of Divinity are more important to us than the Presence to which they point.

Most people do not go beyond fixation with thoughts and words. It would be a grave error to assume words are anything more than a sign pointing in a direction. No matter how divine and sacred the scripture, no matter how holy and revered the spiritual Master,

---

[28] From the book *Awareness - Anthony de Mello Spirituality Conference in His Own Words*

clinging to their words without putting them into practice is like having the remedy for a terminal illness but only reading the label on the bottle three times a day instead of taking the medicine.

I find that I get bored and easily distracted when meditating.

Boredom is nothing more than a label. Many of us are so accustomed to being distracted and stimulated with an overactive mind. Boredom could be considered a withdrawal symptom from the addiction to drama. There has been such a strong addiction to activity, stimulation, thinking, change, or something happening, that sitting silently isn't something that most people are accustomed to.

When you say or think, 'I'm bored." Who is it that is bored? It can only be your *programming* that is bored. When you assume that you are bored you are not witnessing the boredom thoughts, but thinking that those little internal voices are 'me'. With a subtle shift in perspective, you can witness those thoughts like any other and not identify with them.

In more refined states of awareness, it is clear that there is no such thing as a dull or insignificant moment. Boredom no longer exists. Serene contentment effectively calms the ego's incessant need for something to happen, change or be other than what it is.

Is it true that the universe is only an illusion?

The only illusion to be corrected isn't with respect to whether or not the world is real or illusion, but rather the belief that it is somehow separate from Divinity. Concepts of whether the universe is reality or illusion are equally without value. When the tendency to label the world as real or unreal, illusion or not are relinquished, what is left is simply the moment-by-moment experience of life *as it is*. It is not necessary to label it either way.

Changing around labels may seem pleasant and engaging on some level, but such practice will only take you so far down this spiritual path before they become obstacles. Changing the label on a bottle of tomato sauce does not change the taste of it one bit, but this could possibly make things much more complicated at dinnertime than need be.

Perhaps in some teachings, the world has been labelled as illusion for the simple fact that so many lose themselves in it. This may have been intended to inspire one to include spirituality within everyday life. A potential danger lies in rejecting the world, the ego, the self or all that is thought to go under the label 'illusion'. It is <u>not</u> by rejecting something that one is free from it. But only by seeing it as it is.

To some the mind and strong emotions are real and 'me'. But by relating to it differently we come to see that it was only our programming that made it appear so. Our programming turned that rope into a snake. Calling the perceived snake bad or evil does not eliminate our distress! Only seeing the rope for what it is results in true healing.

How can we live without the past?

We don't become utterly oblivious to the past, we just learn how to live without holding onto it. Excessive regret, guilt, sadness, resentment and anger are all signs of clinging to the past. All suffering is an indication of clinging to the past in some form. It is amazing how some people will hold onto petty resentments for decades and never let them go. Forgiveness of self and others is essential to healing emotional distress from the past.

With practice, you can begin to be aware of where you are habitually drawn into past thoughts at the expense of being fully engaged in *this* moment. Awareness of this habit is inevitable and important along this path. It is only when you become conscious of a program that you can begin to actively choose differently.

The self is only a collection of past thoughts. Therefore, it is easy to see that continuing to indulge in unconscious thinking only serves to reinforce the ego.

The mind is very vivid.

To this day, the scent of coffee and cigarette smoke reminds me of visits to my grandparents house when I was a kid. The smell of coffee and cigarettes would instantly teleport me back to having breakfast back at my grandparent's house sitting with my grandfather, listening to him tell me stories of World War II. I would be there completely in my mind. Now the memory can arise, but it doesn't take my attention away from this moment.

Sometimes you see people completely absent. Their eyes may be open but they are clearly not present at all. Oftentimes, a memory will surface and your attention will fade into the past completely. Due to this complete absorption in the field of thought, the mind appears vivid, but only because there is the habit of giving it undue attention.

Is there any value in dream analysis or past life analysis?

These are not necessary for the sake of discovering interior Silence.

What is the value of channelling or channelled material?

There is an endless amount of material that is more likely to add and reinforce illusory beliefs rather than free you from them. The vast majority of channelled material tends to fall under that category. A Course in Miracles is a rare exception to that rule.

Why is it that I always seem to want what I don't have and have what I don't want?

Because the mind is itself the source of all discontent. It perceives lack and projects judgment. Rather than embrace the perfection of what is, the mind tends to reject it.

It is hard to accept the notion that God is everything when the world is filled with nothing but problems and conflict.

Is it wrong that the world appears full of problems and conflict? Or is all unfolding, as it must in the grand scheme of things? Can we always discern what serves the highest good of another? Do we know what path a particular soul chose in order to serve their evolution? These are important questions...

It is humbling to know that there is a bigger picture to all that occurs. Based on the built-in limitations of our judgment and perception we are simply unable to see all ends of any given event. Even though we are not capable of fully knowing the bigger picture, it is enough to know there *is* one. You may see the mess of the world on the news or experience tragedy in your own life and wonder 'why?' or 'why me?' The answer may be too big to process within the confines of the intellect. It could be that everything happens in accordance with a Divine plan that has a purpose on more levels that can be comprehended.

Spiritual growth, the real reason we are all born into this world to begin with, is not always comfortable and convenient. What is good may not always be pleasant. Like gravity, Divinity is pulling us all. The degree of resistance in some makes conflict inevitable. Limiting blind spots in our consciousness may require extreme circumstances to overcome. Often the scenarios that play out in our lives aren't strictly personal. Others may benefit from our experiences and life example.

Recently I read the biography 'Fearless'[29] which outlines the struggles, successes and ultimate sacrifice of Adam Brown, an elite Navy Seal. His tremendous faith carried him through such incredible ordeals. In the end, he gave his life just as he lived it - with fearless dedication. On one hand, his passing at a young age and leaving behind a wife and two young children could be viewed as tragic. On the other hand, the number of people his life has impacted due to his story is awe-inspiring. Who knows if he would have touched as many had he not made the ultimate sacrifice with his life?

The above question is something I too struggled with. What helped me come to terms with the world was identifying what was most important to me in my life. That for me was to know God. Not as someone else told me it should be. Not how I understood it from books or sermons I had heard. Each day I would re-affirm that desire. In each moment, to the best of my ability, I trusted that all that was placed in front of me was the Universe responding to that desire, presenting exactly what is needed in each moment.

---

[29] *Fearless – The Undaunted Courage and Ultimate Sacrafice of Navy Seal Team Six Operator Adam Brown* by Eric Blehm

I've had a very stressful past. Does this put me at a disadvantage for spiritual development?

Your past has brought you to this moment where there is interest in spiritual development. The bus has delivered you to the right place, even if it may appear to have taken a few detours along the way. What is important is where you are going, not where you have come from.

How do I know that I am moving in the right direction? At times I feel stuck and fear I am making no progress.

You have a lifetime of habits that take your attention to anything but inner Silence. Silence is simple but old habits can die slowly. If you suddenly shut off the engine in a freight train moving 85 miles per hour, the train doesn't stop immediately. It continues until the momentum is exhausted. This is similar with the addiction to the mind. Rather than transcending the addiction to it in an instant, it can be a gradual process until the Silence becomes constant and stable.

Even this analogy can be misleading as you may assume that you won't have peace until the mind stops completely. The freedom of Silence is not dependent upon the presence or absence of thought any more than the silence of the sky is dependant upon the presence or absence of birds.

It is mentioned in A Course in Miracles that, 'I see only the past.' Can you elaborate?

All of the experiences of life leave some sort of impact or impression within the nervous system and within the consciousness of each individual. Some of these impressions run deeper than others and can have an emotional charge associated with them that can be painful, stressful or even traumatic. From these, habits are formed based on past experience, which color the experience of the present moment. As these habits are repeated and further reinforced, they become fixtures of perception that are largely unconscious and mostly reactive. All too often, these are naively lumped into the 'this is who I am' category. Thus, there is the erroneous belief that the 'me' or 'I' can be defined by our past.

I remember failing a math test in first grade. As the teacher was handing out the tests during class she held up a paper with a giant 'F' written in bright red that had no name on it and asked the whole class, "Whose is this? Someone forgot to put their name on the paper." With everyone watching, I had to walk to the front of the room to have it handed back to me. It wouldn't have been so bad if most of the papers didn't have a 'B' or 'A' on them with happy face stickers and pleasant comments. Instantly, I believed that I had some defect that made me a bad math student. This carried forth through all of my school years and into college where I avoided majoring in a certain field of study, simply because the math curriculum seemed to be beyond my range of ability. On some level, I never forgot that first test and how others asked me how I could have failed such a simple test. The stress of that moment left an impression that clouded my ability to be innocent with any future math subjects.

It was interesting to notice so many beliefs, even little things from my life that I had picked up along the way and believed to be true, even though they were never my experience. Growing up in a little country town in Oklahoma, we had many pointless arguments on the playground as to which American trucks were the best. Normally these pitted Ford vs. Dodge vs. Chevrolet. One day I found myself arguing on behalf of Chevy and suddenly found the whole tirade to be as hilarious as it was absurd. Here we were, 11 or 12 years old, and none of us had ever even driven a vehicle and yet we had already formed these deep, divisive positions. I would only argue on behalf of a Chevrolet because that is what my dad drove. And ditto for the other playground warring factions representing Ford and Dodge. Through it all, I never saw a single 11 year old Dodge representative sway a Ford advocate to fly a new flag through the war of words. How funny that some of the typical conflicts of humanity can be observed in a playground on pretty much any given day!

Most of us hold as truth things we have been taught by others. We maintain a sense of superiority with respect to the prevalent beliefs and customs of the culture or religion that we were raised in. Few even consider examining their dearly held beliefs and positions due to fear and innocence. Our beliefs become our identity and have to be defended at all costs, otherwise 'I will be offended' or be made wrong or look bad.

Due to the continuous and unconscious projecting of the experiences of the past onto the present, the reality of '*the world as it is*' is distorted into '*the world as I perceive it.*' The common assumption that 'my perception of the universe' represents the genuine article is naive and without merit. While this notion is familiar within modern psychology, the means to complete transcendence of this vicious cycle is not always clear to everyone.

The mind is built of the past. By refusing to indulge in past thinking, it no longer has a leg to stand on. As a result, the reality of *what is* becomes clear. As tranquillity replaces short-sighted assumptions and knee-jerk reactions to the various situations of life, one is less and less inclined to react to situations based on the programming of the past. The need to be right, argue and defend dearly held positions is one glaring example of a reactive pattern based purely on identity with the past. This is done out of the felt need to protect 'who I am.' It is a deterrent along the path of awakening.

As peace begins to prevail over previous habits, the past ceases to bind one into reactive patterns. Within the experience of the world *as it truly is* there is no recognizable value in projecting the past onto anything. Those experiencing life *as it is* see that no part of the universe in and of itself has the power to disturb anyone's peace.   It is only individual consciousness, riddled with altered perceptions that would experience life in this way.

Who am I without my thoughts? Are they not the means by which I create my reality?

It is inaccurate to assume that the mind is 'you' and the source of creativity. The ego lives in constant denial of the source of True Power and therefore claims authorship for it's every thought, feeling and action.

All creativity arises from the Self but is subsequently distorted by the ego until there is the assumption that 'I' did this, thought of that, came up with this idea, etc. As consciousness evolves, this inclination declines. Without the rambling of the mind dominating at every turn, life becomes more spontaneous. The details of life fall into place miraculously. Each day is sufficient unto itself. In the utter simplicity of Silence, there is no worry for what tomorrow may bring and no looking back at the past.

The inventor of the world's first lockstitch sewing machine, Elias Howe Jr., actually perfected his model based on an insight that came to him in a dream where he was captured by cannibals in an African jungle and thrown into a giant pot to boil. Each time he would try to escape they raised their spears and forced him back into the pot. Suddenly he noticed all the spears had a hole in their tips. This provided the missing link that he so desperately sought. The key to an effective working sewing machine stood revealed. Based on this invention, the clothing industry was revolutionized and Mr Howe became the second richest man in the world at the time.

Artists and musicians also describe similar insights of creativity and inspiration. Such moments arise when they are out of the way, letting creativity flow through them. Many of them realize they are only the channels. Just so, the spiritually awakened become channels for the peace of God, each in a unique way.

How will I function in the world if I let go of my mind? Isn't the mind necessary to a certain degree?

At best, the mind is a tool. Normally with any kind of tool, you pick it up and use it when a situation calls for it. When you have finished using a pair of scissors, you put them down. But the mind is a tool that is picked up and rarely put down. There is so much you already do on a day-to-day basis without thinking about it and you don't even realize it. Things like typing on a keyboard, playing a musical instrument, riding a bike, walking, brushing your teeth or driving a car for example don't require thought. They are automatic.

I used to notice that while driving I would be thinking constantly, but not much about driving! The mind is always thinking about something, while attention is seldom given fully to the task at hand. So it is strange to hear anyone ask how he or she will function without the mind when it distracts us so readily as it is.

I could never read a book unless my surroundings were completely quiet. Even in the quiet of a library I would be distracted if someone walked past. I would read a few pages and even though my eyes scanned the pages, I wouldn't register a single word. Before I knew it I was busy thinking about something else. It would take me forever to get through a book! So it was a very welcome change to be able to read in the midst of a busy airport with no problems and no need to re-read a single sentence.

How can I see where I am holding onto limitations?

It is not necessary to spend your time seeking out limitations that are being held. All letting go actually happens as an automatic consequence of applying this practice on a consistent basis. Like a child outgrowing a pair of shoes, consciousness naturally evolves beyond restrictive paradigms. If held long enough limiting positions become painful to maintain.

One example is where victim-based paradigms are transcended. The presumed reality and rewards of playing the victim are recognized as neither reality nor rewarding, but limiting and powerless. Victim behaviour serves to strengthen tendencies of the ego rather than weaken them. I used to blame unhappiness on external causes – "It is this town, school, people, or job." This all changed one day when I noticed that I was feeling down as a direct result of listening to thoughts that were telling me I was angry, sad, etc. It may have been limiting to think this way, but oddly enough it was comfortable to blame something else for how I felt.

With the consistent practice of meditation, such programming fell away. At times, without knowing exactly what changed, my experience of life was suddenly different. I used to play loud, negative music while driving and traffic would be a consistently stressful experience. After a period of regular meditation, I happened to notice that I spent a day running errands around the city, all the while not bothering to turn on the stereo. There was no longer any traffic stress! I was suddenly quite content with quietude inwardly and outwardly. Anxiety that had previously churned constantly beneath the surface had totally disappeared. This extended to all areas of life where I had believed that any disruption of my peace or happiness was most certainly the result of something on the outside.

What are the greatest barriers or blocks to awakening?

The only barrier is the identification with the mind/body/personality as being the true Self. By recognizing clearly what we are *not,* we begin to create distance from it and, in doing so, what you *are* becomes increasingly clear.

All suffering, all perceived differences such as duality, stress, limitation, drama, lack and boredom, are inventions of the mind. Like the reflections on the surface of a pond, the mind actually has no solid reality. It is nothing more than an appearance.

If the addiction to the mind is akin to the darkness of ignorance, Self-Awareness is like shining a light into the darkness. Where light shines there is no darkness to be found. With the light of Awareness, it eventually becomes clear that there is no such thing as the mind. 'Mind' is a concept.

I already feel like a very positive person. Most of my thoughts aren't negative and chaotic. Does this mean I'm free?

Just because thoughts can be positive and pleasant doesn't necessarily mean they will help us expand beyond whatever boundaries we may currently find ourselves in. It is possible to have a pure mind and be a good person, yet still remain unaware of the Silence. A pure attitude that does not include a clear experience of the Self doesn't equal freedom, only a more pleasant relative experience. This is certainly nothing to frown upon at all! Abiding in the Silence is not the result of thinking happy positive thoughts. It requires one to surrender attachment to anything that habitually draws attention away from it.

Some only remember to practice meditation when they are upset. Some only remember it when they are in a good mood. It is commonly assumed that the path of Liberation will be accompanied by feeling eternally happy, which is not accurate. There can even be a period of not feeling much of anything at all! Stillness, joy and bliss are beyond emotions and moods – both negative *and* positive. <u>One must be very cautious in not mistaking a transitory experience for being the supreme state!</u> This can be tricky to discern without help.

By no means does this imply that mental purity is without value. Countless individual testimonials over the years stand as proof of this fact. A shift from negativity to positivity is its own reward in that it brings forth a whole new empowering paradigm of being and opportunities. Recoveries from addictions, as well as transitions from violence to peace are common results. There have even been many miraculous physical and emotional healings that have taken place as one's priority shifts from self-violence to self-acceptance.

Silence is not dependant upon anything that comes and goes - not even the ups and downs of feelings and moods. To assume it is dependant upon a happy or positive thought is an error. *There is not one single condition that it depends upon.* Don't assume that you are far from peace even if you are in complete anguish.

I wish I had heard about this when I was younger. Do all my years of programming and habits make this harder for me?

When you say, "I am this age and therefore I have these limitations," you believe that story is you. Your body can have limitations. It will age, fall ill, become injured but the real 'you' is timeless. This thought can become an excuse as to why you cannot live in joy now. Don't allow your mind to create a process out of this practice. It will always find some reason that you cannot be at Peace now.

How do your values change as you grow?

Love and compassion gradually replace previous

internal programs and motivations. True love and compassion are impersonal and effortless. As the obstructions of the ego dissolve, these radiate outward as effortlessly as fragrance from a flower.

Why is it so difficult to live in the present moment?

This is only the result of deeply ingrained habit. The present moment doesn't elude anyone. We are just accustomed to focusing on thoughts that take us elsewhere. By focusing on the clouds, it appears as though the sun is elusive. Only the mind moves, Reality stays put. Life out of the present moment is only imagined.

What are some of the external characteristics of a Mystic?

One cannot go by external signs to determine the inner state of the mystic with certainty. Sometimes those who appear saintly are far from it. And, just as well, those who you may not expect it from may experience a profound relationship with the Divine. The saintly can appear very ordinary, while deception can wear a very clever and convincing mask.

Some may attract large audiences and committed students while others may live in solitude and relative obscurity. They may blend into the crowd and appear to live an ordinary life. Many are the sages the world has never known. Popularity is not a clear-cut sign of authenticity. Consider the many cults just in the last century that have led droves of people astray in the worst of ways – many well-known cases resulted in spiritual disillusionment and even death.

Even today, countless students hand power over to groups and individuals in the name of spiritual advancement. This is potentially quite dangerous. A true teacher will want nothing from their students. And yet they will do whatever they can to make their teachings clear and understandable. Even so, there is no investment in others 'getting it'. Nothing is added to their awareness of the Divine by others agreeing with them, and nothing is taken away from their awareness of the Divine by others disagreeing with them. There is giving and sharing without attachment. Consider the example of Jesus washing the feet of his disciples. It was an act of pure love and service without seeking anything in return. Nobody who experiences absorption in Divinity can be anything but humble.

Some internal qualities that a true mystic embodies are worth noting. Far from being mere personality traits, these qualities are innate to the state in which the mystic abides. Not all who discover internal

Silence are going to act the same way by any means. As the state itself has been described throughout this book already, we can add here that those who are absorbed in the Divine do not experience *neediness*. So any motivation to control, take or get something from others – whether that be money, approval, popularity, emotional attachment, adoration, sex, attention, love, etc. – would probably come from a place of lack. Why would one who is purportedly full and complete within themselves need to take anything from their students? The motivation for gain must mean that happiness is still dependant upon conditions. This is a sign that one is not free from the fetters of the ego-self.

Many false teachers act out how they believe an enlightened being would be. This can take the form of odd clothing, pious sounding platitudes, pregnant pauses while speaking, glazed over stares and power over all the details of their student's life. Some even dictate what brand of clothing or household products their students should buy! This is meddling in the everyday affairs of others to a very unhealthy degree. Some false teachers charge extraordinary amounts of money and make guarantees on spiritual advancement. This is a definite a red flag as nobody can guarantee how enlightened you will be in x number of days, months or years. Nobody can give another spiritual enlightenment! It is not a 'thing' to be transferred from point a. to point b. Some charge hefty fees to transfer enlightenment to their students.[30] This is a clear sign that the teacher does not have a clue what spiritual enlightenment really is. A classic case of the blind leading the blind.

A true mystic does not even care whether they have an audience or not. When necessary, a spiritual teacher or organization may charge a fee in order to cover expenses just as any business would. So the exchange of money is not an automatic smoke-signal of impurity. Some spiritual teachers reap a fortune for themselves and the whole spiritual thing becomes a lucrative endeavour where gain becomes the prime motive. Many so-called spiritual teachers have successfully marketed themselves by selling pure fantasy and untruth. Many flock to the next big thing, hoping to attain that special pie-in-the-sky experience that they feel will make them whole.

It may be believed that a mystical state is like an upgrade to your current state of being. This is not so. Absorption in Silence means the dissolution of the part which believes in lack and therefore seeks gain. It is the dissolution of the belief in an individual 'I' that

---

[30] Such as via 'diksha' or 'shaktipat'

stands apart from the source of the greatest Fullness until only Fullness remains.

To the mystic, Divine Absorption is full and complete in each moment. All of life in all its minute details is embraced as the unfolding of God's Will. Given that fact, the mystic will not whine and complain or fall into victim-based programming. While their personalities may differ widely, all mystics abide in a state of profound Joy and Peace. What separates the mystic from anyone else? They see the dream of suffering as a dream, while those who do not experience this Peace and Joy believe the dream of suffering to be reality.

The teachings of Sri Ramana Maharshi rank among the greatest sources of inspiration in my life. In the late 1800's, while only a teenager, Ramana experienced a sudden awakening and lived the remainder of his life absorbed in unbroken identity with the Silence. During those years, countless aspirants came to visit him from all over the world. Even though he spoke little, if at all, many were inspired and enlivened just by sitting in his presence. Initially, Ramana had no idea what had happened that day as a teenager, he only knew there was no longer identification with what he had previously believed himself to be – the mind/body/personality. Profound

Silence remained as the 'I' or primary identity. It was only later when he had read and heard accounts of other awakened beings, that he realised he was already experiencing what they had described.

In spite of his enormous worldwide popularity, Maharshi owned next to nothing. On a video documentary about his life,[31] he is seen sitting still and unmoving for long periods even as flies landed and crawled over his face. On top of that he never bothered with much clothing as he wandered around with a walking stick wearing only a loincloth.

After seeing this, I instantaneously adopted the belief that this was how spiritual enlightenment looked. Even though I wanted to experience what he had come to realize more than anything, I was also reluctant for fear that I would one day wander out of the house in my underwear. I would not have lasted long in the harsh Wyoming winter!

After exploring the teachings and teachers of other traditions, at times I was tempted to mimic what I thought enlightenment was. While I am happy to say this never resulted in a wardrobe of loincloths, it did result in a new collection of 'enlightened' concepts. I believed I would become something different or look

---

[31] Videos on Ramana Maharshi can be easily found on the Internet.

a certain way. All ideas of how we feel we should be or act are presumptions that do not necessarily represent reality. If you prefer chocolate ice cream and warm sunny days before enlightenment, who is to say that this would be different after enlightenment?

It is transformational to drop our notions of how holiness must appear. This wonderful story speaks volumes about how perception can easily shift in an instant and bring about a much more enlivening set of circumstances.

'The abbot of a once famous Buddhist monastery that had fallen into decline was deeply troubled. Monks were lax in their practice, novices were leaving and lay supporters deserting to other centers. He traveled far to a sage and recounted his tale of woe, of how much he desired to transform his monastery to the flourishing haven it had been in days of yore.

The sage looked him in the eye and said, "The reason your monastery has languished is that the Buddha is living among you in disguise, and you have not honored Him." The abbot hurried back, his mind in turmoil.

The Selfless One was at his monastery! Who could He be? Brother Hua?...No, he was full of sloth. Brother Po?...No, he was too dull. But then the

Tathagata was in disguise. What better disguise than sloth or dull- wittedness? He called his monks to him and revealed the sage's words. They, too, were taken aback and looked at each other with suspicion and awe.

Which one of them was the Chosen One?

The disguise was perfect. Not knowing who He was they took to treating everyone with the respect due to a Buddha. Their faces started shining with an inner radiance that attracted novices and then lay supporters.

In no time at all the monastery far surpassed its previous glory.'[32]

What kind of effect does one have on humanity as they evolve in conscious awareness?

Whether positive or negative, each of our thoughts, feelings and actions affects the whole of creation. Each gesture that is rooted in praise, gratitude, love and compassion uplifts all of mankind. If there is unwavering dedication to Truth and your life is wrapped around that sole dedication, then it is

---

[32] Dr. Mitchell Gibson

possible to dedicate every thought, word and deed to the greater Good in all that you do.

Some years ago I was made aware of a particular way of viewing my meditation practice that totally changed the way I looked at myself from that moment onward. The practice is this –

During your practice of meditation,[33] choose to view each of your thoughts and experiences as more than just yours. What if a jealousy issue you were struggling with was merely a jealousy issue that existed in the collective consciousness of all humanity? What if by transcending that within yourself, you made it more likely that countless others on the planet would be able to do the same? What if moving beyond a 'busy mind' and into peace wasn't just about you? What if each time you made the effort to move beyond it, that likelihood was enhanced in the collective to such a degree that others would follow suit? What if each time a program of depression arose, you could see it as just an echo within the collective? That the energy field of 'depression' was enhanced by millions of others caught in it? What if all your efforts to move beyond it helped all the ones who remained at its mercy? In this way, your meditation practice becomes

---

[33] Which ideally is continuous.

a service to all of humanity. Everything that arises within your awareness is an opportunity to heal it for others. No matter what addiction or issue you happen to be dealing with, far from being just a clever example, it is actually the truth of the matter. Much of what we experience is not 'ours' much less 'us' even if it feels like it is.

It is our dedication to the great spiritual teachings and principles that makes the difference. Ghandi's movement of non-violence was the result of his unwavering dedication to non-violence in his own life. His dedication to truth never wavered even in the face of extreme violence and oppression. The subsequent impact upon millions of people stands as an example to the power of pure, unwavering commitment to truth.

Each individual that steps beyond the bounds of negativity and separation makes it easier for others to follow. Each person that finds their way out of a dense jungle leaves a trail for others to follow. If only a few had traversed the path to freedom, the trail can be obscure and yet each person that realises freedom leaves their indelible mark on it. As a result, the path of enlightenment becomes easier and easier for the next person to recognise and follow.

There was a time when it was believed to be next to impossible for a human to be able to run a mile in under four minutes. Yet the first time somebody accomplished the feat, it didn't take long for others to follow. The first time someone flew a plane across the Atlantic Ocean another barrier fell. These monumental moments made headlines around the world. Nowadays, who can say how many flights cross the Atlantic on a daily basis? The seemingly miraculous has become the norm.

These are obvious examples that were visible to the world. Within the invisible domain of pure consciousness, each thought, feeling and action also leaves a permanent imprint within the all-pervading field of consciousness. An individual's addiction to the ego reinforces humanities stubborn addiction to the ego. Each soul that aligns with truth reinforces that for the collective. Every single thought, feeling and action that is devoted to God, facilitates the greater likelihood that others will follow in the wake of that devotion. It is inspiring to know that spiritual commitment isn't only about you. The spiritually committed serve all humanity often without even knowing it at times. Devotion to discovering God within is the single most powerful, worthwhile and effective thing that one can do for the world.

PART IV

Fulfilling Divine Potential By Being the Change

Many who devote themselves to spiritual work may become increasingly sensitive to the suffering of others. This can lead one to seek ways to help foster positive change in the world. Motivation could arise to follow the example of a great soul such as Mother Teresa, Gandhi or Martin Luther King. This is without doubt a noble endeavour. And yet, if we believe our contribution must look a certain way, this can limit us.

To avoid this, it is important to remain open to what the Universe presents in response to your intentions. Sometimes what is held in mind will happen as envisioned, but sometimes it will not. Perhaps we would like to preach to the masses, but maybe God has another plan for how we could best serve the greater good for all. If we get too heavily invested in one particular way coming to fruition, we get in the way of the flow of Grace working through us.

Gandhi once said, *"We must be the change we wish to see in the world."* If you want to see peace and non-violence in the world, it would be wise to culture that within ourselves first. If you want to see love, become the most unconditionally loving being that you can. If you want to see common courtesy and generosity then be the one who does that in all moments. We can all choose to be the best example of what we wish to see.

Sometimes a grandiose vision of how we think we should 'be the change' keeps us from fully enjoying and embracing what life presents to us in each moment. It is possible to place unnecessary pressure on ourselves to live up to a potentially unrealistic ideal. However noble, we may wind up getting trapped in a spiritualized version of *my will*. It can be difficult to recognize a position of *my will* when there is a big shiny halo wrapped around it.

Mother Teresa offers a profound piece of advice when she suggests 'doing little things with great Love'[34]. It is often easy to overlook the little things and believe they aren't as significant or good enough. Rather than embracing each moment fully, it is tempting to look for something in the future that will match our preconceived notions.

What if each and every thing we are faced with, no matter how seemingly insignificant, *is* our opportunity

---

[34] *Where There is Love there is God* by Mother Teresa

to impact change, both within ourselves and throughout the world simultaneously? What if all our attempts to overcome addictions to approval, to alcohol, to sadness or jealousy, benefit everyone else on the planet who struggles with the exact same problems? The ego-self would love to think its issues are isolated unto itself. It does not even consider that each person who moves beyond any sort of conflict within themselves does it for everyone else. The fact that we may be unaware of this does not change this fact.

Obviously, not every saint and sage has been in the public eye. They most often work anonymously behind the scenes. They choose to read the script that God has written for them rather than attempting to bend and shape it to fit an idealistic notion.

Everything life presents can be embraced with great love and respect if you see it as a gift from God. There is no such thing as an insignificant moment. Not a single one of your prayers and wishes to grow in awareness and/or be of assistance in this world goes unnoticed. Even the simple act of being faced with a busy mind in meditation can be seen as a gift. *My will* wanted the surface chatter to calm down, but instead finds more than normal. *My will* wanted a smooth trip home, but instead finds itself stuck in traffic. *My will* complains and moans when it isn't getting its way.

If you desire to grow spiritually and impact change, then take heart - your wish is granted already. There is no such thing as independent and personal enlightenment isolated from the rest of the world. Each baby step of the greenest spiritual beginner is already impacting the whole. Even the greatest of saints had to begin somewhere. Earnest effort is supported by the universe and the universe benefits in turn. The saints, sages and mystics were once subjected to beliefs of separation and suffering just like the rest of us. Without experiencing this initially, they wouldn't have the clarity to become teachers for those caught in the snares of ego-mind.

Some wise advice comes from a favorite quote of mine, *'It is better to travel well than to arrive.'*[35] Sometimes we get so caught up in where we think we should be, that we miss the beauty of what is right in front of us. What are the most common characteristics of the mystic? They fully enjoy and embrace each moment. They realize that in the Silence of our true essence, *all is well.* And when all is seen as the Will of God, where is there room for sorrow?

---

[35] This quote is most often attributed to Buddha.

'Let the Tao become present in your life and you will become genuine. Let it be present in your family and your family will flourish. Let it be present in your country and your country will be an example to all countries in the world. Let it be present in the universe and the universe will sing. How do I know this? By looking inside myself.' [36]

---

[36] *Tao Te Ching* by Stephen Mitchell

Dabblers vs. Doers

This book is an open invitation for you to have your own experience. The means have been outlined clearly with the Technique and the Five Steps. If you take nothing else from reading this, then at the very least, you have a simple method that can be applied anytime, anywhere and in any situation. It will work wonders whether you believe it will or not. Of itself, the practice is supremely simple, so simple that it can be deceiving at times. Take care not to complicate it in any way. You may wonder, "Could a simple practice like this really make that big of a difference?" There is only one way to find out.

For the practice offered in this book to be most effective, a brief glance or a little bit of casual dabbling here and there will not suffice. Consistent use as instructed is recommended. Eyes open and eyes closed practice can be easily incorporated into a daily routine. This will not interfere with daily life. After all, the mind is constantly moving with random thoughts all the time. The technique offers a new direction for consciousness to move. If you desire to experience Internal Silence as described throughout this book, then it must be made a priority. This is not a passive teaching.

After years of meditation, I am amazed at the power and simplicity of it all. I am equally amazed at how some people who attend workshops, retreats receive the simplest tools, stop using them after a short while. They may not be happy to be drifting around in the choppy seas of thought, but neither do they use the tools they have. Why let a perfectly good tool collect rust? If you have a remedy for the illness, it is worthless if it is never used.

One summer while on break from university, I worked a construction job rebuilding roofs. On payday our checks were brought to us on the roof as we worked. My first check for a week of physically demanding labor was just under $300. I remember receiving it in the midst of a busy day on the rooftop of an elementary school. Naturally I didn't want to lose it, so I tucked it into the front pocket of my shirt and snapped the button closed. The rest of the day I hardly let my attention waver from that check, knowing full well I would not get another if I lost it. I was able to go about my day and do what I needed to do. But in all the busyness, my attention rarely wavered from that check for more than a brief instant here and there. It was not at all difficult to do this.

Years later, when I began meditating I suffered from 'monkey mind'. My attention would drift and wander from the practice oh so easily! Then I remembered that day with the check and it helped put things into perspective. I was so willing to maintain gentle and consistent awareness on a $300 check, but when it came to directing attention onto my meditation practice I became careless. Did I value the Divine within more than that check? Of course! So it wasn't that I was unable to stay consistently aware. It would be more accurate to say that I had just become lazy about it. I remember complaining how hard it was at times. Then, I chose to let that go. When I noticed attention had wavered, I silently and swiftly returned it to the practice without all the undue commentary, without looking back or berating myself. It may seem like a tug of war battle at times, but always find ways to be simple and easy. That is your choice. Put in the effort, but leave behind the forcefulness.

Dabbling is great for trying out lots of things, learning a little bit about many different practices. But only those who commit to doing the work will see actual progress. This is so with anything. The Taj Mahal was not built by a dabbler. Those who become doctors are not dabblers in their course work. No true mystic realized freedom by casually peeking at their practice from time to time.

One reason for dabbling can be due to the fact that clarity on exactly which practice or teaching to use has yet to become apparent. But switching from one path to another is also the hallmark of the perpetual seeker. Perpetual seeking could very well be listed as a trap of the spiritual ego. It is threatening to the ego-mind to commit to a practice and stay the course. The spiritual pack rat gathers a multitude of information and tends to remain in a comfort zone as they accumulate vast intellectual understanding. While they gather much, they commit to nothing. The real work of un-doing the mechanisms of the ego's programming have yet to be undertaken in any significant way.

Greatness is reserved for the committed and is not a reward from God. Internal Peace is not caused by spiritual practice – it is revealed. Recovery from any addiction comes with dedication to sobriety and all that it takes to get there. For those who persevere, the result is never regretted. Liberation is not *caused* by adhering to a practice any more than a gardener *causes* his plants to thrive. A wise gardener simply presents the appropriate conditions and growth flourishes of its own. And so it is with awareness.

"May you always walk in beauty" [37]

---

[37] Native American prayer.

WORKS CITED

A Beautiful Mind. Dir. Ron Howard. Dreamworks, 2001.

Blehm, Eric. *Fearless: The Undaunted Courage and Ultimate Sacrifice of Navy Seal Team Six Operator Adam...* [S.l.]: Waterbrook Pr, 2013. Print.

Bruce, Robert. *Astral Dynamics: The Complete Book of Out-of-body Experiences.* Charlottesville, VA: Hampton Roads Pub., 2009. Print.

Buhlman, William. *Adventures beyond the Body: How to Experience Out-of-body Travel.* [San Francisco, Calif.]: HarperSanFrancisco, 1996. Print.

Caussade, Jean Pierre De. *The Joy of Full Surrender.* Brewster, MA: Paraclete, 2008. Print.

A Course in Miracles: The Text, Workbook for Students and Manual for Teachers. New York: Viking, 1996. Print.

de Mello Anthony, and J. Francis. Stroud.

Awareness: A De Mello Spirituality Conference in His Own Words. New York: Doubleday, 1990. Print.

de Mello, Anthony, S.J. *Taking Flight: A Book of Story Meditations*. New York, NY: Image, 1990. Print.

Eckhart, Edmund Colledge, and Bernard McGinn. *Meister Eckhart, the Essential Sermons, Commentaries, Treatises, and Defense*. New York: Paulist, 1981. Print.

Eknath, Easwaran, trans. *The Dhammapada*. Tomales, CA: Nilgiri, 2007. Print.

Huang Po. *The Zen Teaching of Huang Po on the Transmission of Mind: Being the Teaching of the Zen Master Huang Po*. Trans. John Blofeld. New York: Grove, 1958. Print.

Kramer, Joel, and Diana Alstad. *The Guru Papers: Masks of Authoritarian Power*. Berkeley, CA: North Atlantic /Frog, 1993. Print.

Lamsa, George M. *Holy Bible: From the Ancient Eastern Text*. [San Francisco]: HarperSanFrancisco,

1985. Print.

Millemon, Chad. *Ascension Meditation: An Introduction and Guidebook.* [S.l.]: Mystic Way Publishing, 2013. Print.

Prabhavananda, comp. *The Upanishads, Breath of the Eternal: The Principle Texts Selected and Translated from the Original Sanskrit.* Trans. Frederick Manchester. New York: New American Library, 1957. Print.

Ramana, Maharshi, and David Godman. *Be as You Are: The Teachings of Sri Ramana Maharshi.* New Delhi: Penguin, 1992. Print.

Śaṅkarācārya, Prabhavananda, and Christopher Isherwood. *Shankara's Crest-jewel of Discrimination = Viveka-chudamani.* Hollywood, CA: Vedanta, 1978. Print.

Teresa, Mother, and Brian Kolodiejchuk. *Where There Is Love, There Is God: A Path to Closer Union with God and Greater Love for Others.* New York: Image, 2012. Print.

ABOUT THE AUTHOR

Chad Millemon has taught worldwide since 1999. In addition to instructing beginner courses, he has also guided extended in-residence retreats with advanced students from a wide variety of cultural backgrounds and from all walks of life.

After discovering that meditation and spirituality were not at all complicated, but amazingly simple, Chad has chosen to share his insights with others who seek clarity within their own lives. Even though he belongs to no specific tradition or lineage he offers instruction in a wide variety of formats to people of all faiths.

Chad currently resides with his wife Carolyn in Wyoming.

For additional information about the author, the
books, workshops, lectures, meditation classes and
retreats feel free to contact **info@mysticwaypub.com**
or visit **www.mysticwaypub.com**

Mystic Way